EVERY SIXTH ISRAELI

Relations Between the Jewish Majority
and the Arab Minority in Israel

EVERY SIXTH ISRAELI

Relations Between the Jewish Majority
and the Arab Minority in Israel

Editor

Alouph Hareven

THE VAN LEER JERUSALEM FOUNDATION
JERUSALEM

ISBN 965–271–001–6

Translated from the Hebrew edition

Typeset and printed in Israel by Daf-Chen Press, Jerusalem

CONTENTS

Chapter I: Introduction

Chapter II: To Be an Arab in a Jewish State — Personal Testimonies

Chapter III: Minority and Majority: The Problem of Integration

Chapter IV: The Problem of Education

Chapter V: The Identity Problem of the Arab Minority

Chapter VI: The Essential Problem: What Should Be the Mutual Relations Between Majority and Minority in a Jewish State?

Chapter I

INTRODUCTION

THE ARABS OF ISRAEL:
A JEWISH PROBLEM

ALOUPH HAREVEN

> Of the crucial questions arising from the idea of our people's rebirth on its land, there is one equal in importance to all the rest taken together, namely, the question of our relation to the Arabs. The hope for our national revival depends on the proper solution of that question, which has not been forgotten but has simply vanished ... That it has been possible to divert attention from such a fundamental issue and that after thirty years of settlement activity it must be spoken of as if it was a newly discovered subject — that sad fact is proof enough of the superficiality of mind prevailing in our movement; it shows that we are still skimming over the surface of issues and do not get down to their core and essence.
>
> Yitzhak Epstein, "She'ela Ne'elama"
> ("An Unseen Question")
> *Hashiloah,* 1906.

No person or group can claim exclusive title to the condition of being a minority. Practically everyone in the course of his lifetime has had some kind of minority experience — as a child, an adult or an elderly person; by being outstanding or deficient in some field of endeavor; by having a surfeit of rights, or by being deprived of them. All the parties in the Knesset from the time of the establishment of Israel until now (1983) have been minority parties; none of them has ever obtained a majority. As long as they live in the Diaspora, the Jews will remain a minority. Democratic countries, where minorities can express their views without fear, are a minority in the world and in the United Nations.

So too, one out of six persons in Israel belong to a minority, a non-Jewish minority in a Jewish state, the Arabs of Israel. In 1948 they numbered 156,000 and comprised 18 percent of the population. In 1982 they numbered 650,000, or 16 percent of the population. In 1993 they will number about one million and will comprise about 20 percent of the population (one out of five). Already today 75 percent of them are Israelis by birth, that is, they were born in Israel after the establishment of the state, grew up and received their education in Israel. It is a younger population than the Jewish majority: the mean age of the Jews in Israel is 30, of the non-Jews, 21. It is also a fertile population: its rate of annual natural increase is 38 per thousand as compared to 18 per thousand among the Jews.

The size of the non-Jewish minority in Israel today equals that of the Jewish population in Israel in its first year. In that year — 1948 — the Declaration of Independence stipulated that the State of Israel "will ensure complete equality of social and political rights to all its citizens irrespective of religion, race or sex; it will guarantee freedom of religion, conscience, language, education and culture ...".

The figures speak for themselves. In the population as a whole the minority are one in six. In the Ninth Knesset they were one in seventeen. The Government Yearbook of 1978 lists the names of 2,287 Jews in senior government positions, as compared to only 37 non-Jews, or one out of sixty. In Israel's universities there are about 6,000 Jews in academic positions, and about 20

Arabs: one out of three hundred. There has never been an Arab Supreme Court justice. No large economic institution in Israel is headed by an Arab — no bank, industrial enterprise or agricultural undertaking. In one area alone the situation is somewhat different: one out of ten members of the Histadrut are Arabs, as are one out of sixteen of the members of the Histadrut Executive Committee.

Numbers are a quantitative expression of a given situation. There are undoubtedly some who regard these figures as a considerable achievement: they show how in the course of its first generation Israel succeeded in maintaining its distinctiveness as a Jewish state. Others undoubtedly view these figures as an indication of failure: they prove that the Jews, who have traditionally fought for their rights as a minority, are now failing to accord such rights fully to the minority living in their midst. And certainly there are many others who would argue that ours is an abnormal situation; we ourselves are a minority among a hundred million Arabs; why should we endanger ourselves by according full rights to the Arabs among us when their brethren are threatening our very existence?

As long as the Arab-Israeli conflict was total, that kind of argument had a good deal of force. But since 1979 we have been officially at peace with a country of forty million Arabs, and the sixty thousand Israelis who have already visited Egypt have returned surprised by the lack of animosity they encountered there. The conflict can no longer serve as a general and ready excuse for our treatment of the Arab minority. How, then, shall we regard this problem?

We can view it as an Arab problem; that is, a problem for which the Arabs themselves must find a solution, and which is not at all the concern of the Jews. Many Jews undoubtedly favor that approach, for it exempts them from having to deal with a discomfiting problem. However, it does not absolve them of the responsibility for the consequences of their refusal to deal with it.

The predicament of Israel's Arabs may also be regarded as a

Jewish problem, starting with what the Jews in Israel actually know — and do not know — about the problems of the minority. It appears that most of the Jewish population neither knows nor wants to know what this entails. That is understandable. It is as if to say: "Are we so lacking in problems in this country that on top of everything else you want to impose on us the problems of one out of six Israelis? We have more than our share with war, inflation, social gaps, unemployment, crime, unattainable housing, uneven balance of payments, populating the Negev and the Galilee, establishing settlements. Don't pile additional problems on us!"

To this history and human nature have provided a simple answer: whoever ignores a problem, will eventually be surprised by it. Relations between the Jewish majority and the Arab minority will inevitably be one of the critical issues in the second generation of Israel's existence.

II

In the interaction between the two groups, it is the Jewish majority which has the power to decide matters, to examine its treatment and perception of the Arab minority, and then to consider whether we are satisfied with it, or whether it warrants change.

A survey of the attitudes of Israel's Jews towards the Arab minority, conducted in 1980 for The Van Leer Jerusalem Foundation by Mina Tsemach, revealed the following.

● *The majority of Jews in Israel are ambivalent in their attitudes towards Israeli Arabs.* There exist among the Jewish community three main groups: a minority whose attitudes towards Israeli Arabs are mainly negative; another minority whose attitudes are mainly positive, and in between the two a group comprising the majority of Jews in Israel, whose attitudes to Israeli Arabs are ambivalent.

● *The group attributing to Israeli Arabs only negative characteristics comprises 14% of the respondents.* This group consists mainly of Jews originating from Arab countries, 18–22-year-old Jews, and persons who voted for the Likud and the National Religious parties (though, of course, not all persons belonging to those categories are totally negative in their attitudes towards Arabs). As we stated, this is a minority group, compared with which 84% of Jews in Israel have different attitudes — either positive, or mixed.

● *The Jewish group attributing to Israeli Arabs only positive traits consists of 13% of the respondents.* This too is a minority group among the Jewish population, and outstanding among it are persons originating in the West, native-born Israelis whose parents immigrated from the West, persons with higher education, and persons living in cities where there is also an Arab population.

● *The largest group* — comprising 70% of Jews in Israel, is the one in which mixed attitudes prevail. Persons in this group may attribute to Israeli Arabs some positive traits (such as being diligent, being devoted to one's family) as well as some negative traits (such as being violent).

● *The complexity* of Jewish attitudes can be perceived through the following findings: "The Arab is dirty" — 36% think so, "clean" or "neither clean nor dirty" — 64%; "The Arab is devoted to his family" — 69%; "not devoted to his family" — 9% (the remaining responses are somewhere between the two poles); "the Arab values human life" — 42%; "does not value human life" — 33%; "most Israeli Arabs are spies" — 16%; "most Israeli Arabs are glad when Israel is harmed" — 53% of Jews think so; other opinions — 47%; "most Israeli Arabs are torn between their loyalty to the State and their loyalty to the Arab people" — 45%; other opinions — 55%.

● *The survey reveals internal tensions among the attitudes of the Jewish community.* For example, the tension between the basic attitude of 90% of the respondents, about the need to practice tolerance towards minority groups, wherever they may be, and the willingness of only 40% to grant equal rights to the Arab minority in Israel. The main justification of those opposing

the full application of equal rights is based on security consider-
ations.

● As against those tensions one of the most encouraging findings concerns the willingness of Jews to establish social contacts
with Israeli Arabs. About 40% are willing to live in the same
apartment house; more than half of the respondents are willing
to establish social contacts with Arabs in their city; about 60%
are prepared to work with Arabs. These findings indicate that a
considerable part of the Jewish community *do not have racist
attitudes* towards Israeli Arabs; that is, they have no reservations
about contacts with Israeli Arabs, such as whites in South Africa
may have vis-à-vis the blacks. Quite to the contrary, the high
ratio of Jews willing to establish social contacts with Arabs probably indicates a potential for normal relations, which has not yet
been realized. This high ratio is important, because surveys conducted among Israeli Arabs have revealed that among them, too,
there exists a high ratio of persons with interest in establishing
social relations with Jews; however, the ratio of Israeli Arabs
who believe that Jews are willing to establish such relations is low.

Practical conclusions arising from this survey are on the following levels:

● The prevailing impression that the attitude of most Jews in
Israel towards Israeli Arabs is basically negative — is erroneous.
The number of Jews in Israel whose attitudes towards Israeli
Arabs are so negative that they can be described as racist does
not exceed 15%, or three out of every twenty Jews. One can
hope that whoever wishes Israel to survive both as a democracy
and as a Jewish state upholding the rights of minorities in accordance with Jewish tradition will explicitly define himself as *outside*
this small group, and will do his utmost to contain its influence.

● The attitudes of the Jewish majority in Israel contain positive elements which can be brought to bear in reducing negative
attitudes and improving the general posture towards Arabs who
are Israeli citizens. Such activity is important especially in the
field of education. So far, the Jewish educational system has not

offered any program teaching Jewish pupils how to relate to one sixth of the citizens of Israel who are not Jewish. The absence of such a program is possibly one of the reasons why attitudes among Jewish youth towards Israeli Arabs are more negative than among various adult groups. While in many countries young people are the group which reveals empathy with the condition of minority groups, it appears that in Israel the situation is reversed. Both Jewish and Arab youth show disquieting indications of mutual intolerance. Recognizing this deficiency, the Ministry of Education established, in 1982, a committee charged with planning the education of Arab and Jewish pupils, throughout twelve years of schooling, on the relations between Arabs and Jews as equal citizens.*

● There are ample findings in the survey to strengthen the view that it may be possible to develop majority-minority relations in Israel based on mutual respect of civil rights even where there is dissension on the solution of outstanding political problems. The initiative must come from the Jewish majority. The Jews' idea of what Israeli Arabs think of them is based largely on our own attitude to the Arab minority. The more we reinforce negative stereotypes ("dirty," "spies") the more we strengthen negative elements in their attitude to us. And the more we strengthen existing positive elements in the attitude of parts of the Jewish majority, the more we increase the Israeli Arabs' consciousness of being equal citizens of Israel.

At least partial confirmation of the assumption that the attitude of Israeli Arabs to the State and to the Jewish majority is, to some extent, a reflection of Jewish attitudes towards them, can be found in a survey conducted recently by Dr. Sammy Smooha of Haifa University. The survey was carried out in July 1980, among a representative sample of 1185 Israeli Arabs. At the request of The Van Leer Jerusalem Foundation, it also included

* In 1982, The Van Leer Jerusalem Foundation, together with the Ministry of Education, produced the first experimental edition on relations between Arabs and Jews in Israel, for secondary schools.

several questions which where parallel to those in the survey carried out among Jews. What follows are a few comparisons between the two surveys:

● To the question *do Arabs in Israel hate Jews*, the replies were:

Answer	Percentage of replies among Jewish respondents		Percentage of replies among Arab respondents	
Affirmative in regard to most Israeli Arabs	22.6	51.6	7.2	29.1
Affirmative in regard to a large group among them	25.0		21.9	
Affirmative in regard to a certain group among them	32.1		31.1	
Affirmative in regard to a small group among them	10.2	18.7	21.4	39.8
Affirmative in regard to a few or none	8.5		18.4	

● To the question *have Israeli Arabs reconciled themselves to the existence of Israel*, the replies were:

Answer	Percentage of replies among Jewish respondents		Percentage of replies among Arab respondents	
Affirmative in regard to most Israeli Arabs	11.7	29.2	40.4	67.7
Affirmative in regard to a large group among them	17.5		27.3	
Affirmative in regard to a certain group among them	23.5		16.9	
Affirmative in regard to a small group among them	22.6	46.4	9.1	15.4
Affirmative in regard to a few or none	23.8		6.3	

A comparison of the answers of Jews and Arabs to each question reveals that Jews tend to attribute to Israeli Arabs positions far more extreme than Israeli Arabs tend to attribute to themselves (even when we assume that a certain part of the Arab respondents distorted their answers deliberately so as to hide their negative feelings).

The assumption about a possible distortion of Arab replies is largely refuted when we compare the answers of Arabs on their attitude to Israeli leaders and institutions:

● Arab respondents were asked to *what extent they were satisfied with each of the personalities and institutions listed below.* The following is the breakdown of their answers (in percentage of Arab replies).

From these answers it becomes obvious that Israeli Arabs do differentiate, in their attitudes, among different personalities and institutions in Israel, and that they do not hesitate to express their differentiation, both positively and negatively. Thus, 55.1% are *satisfied* with President Navon, as against 65.6% who are *dissatisfied* with Prime Minister Begin; only 36.7% are satisfied with the Knesset, 37.2% with Israeli democracy and 33% with freedom of speech; but 58.2% are satisfied with the legal system and 90.1% with the medical services.

Such findings should be sufficient to put us on guard against simplistic and stereotypical views regarding the attitude of Israeli Arabs to Israel and to its Jews. Their attitudes are complex and multi-dimensional, and to a large extent the Arabs respond to us as we respond to them. Therefore, the critical question which the Jewish majority faces is: where, among us, are the foci of intolerance which influence the attitudes of the Jewish majority, and the responding attitudes of the Arab minority? The survey by Mina Tsemach clearly indicates that the higher rates of intolerance towards Arabs who are Israeli citizens are to be found among Jews with a low level of education, among Jews originating from Arab countries, among those who vote for the Likud and for the Mafdal,* or, if we may hazard a conjecture, among

---

* National Religious Party.

Extent of Satisfaction of Arab Respondents with Personalities and Institutions

Extent of satisfaction	With President Navon	With Prime Minister Begin	With the Knesset	With Israeli democracy	With freedom of speech in Israel	With the legal system	With Israeli medical services
Very satisfied	22.5	3.4	9.4	10.5	11.3	16.7	51.2
	55.1	14.4	36.7	37.2	33.9	58.2	90.1
Satisfied	32.6	11.0	27.3	26.7	21.7	41.5	38.9
Indifferent	28.5	12.9	12.0	12.0	10.7	16.7	2.8
Dissatisfied	7.8	27.3	21.8	30.2	30.7	14.7	4.8
	16.3	65.6	48.2	50.8	53.1	25.1	7.2
Completely dissatisfied	8.5	48.3	26.4	20.6	22.4	10.4	2.4

persons for whom religion and nation are supreme values which perceive the treatment of a minority as though their rights were inferior.

The question which the Jewish majority must ask itself is whether its leaders and its educational system do encourage the Israeli people — both majority and minority — to practice that measure of tolerance and equality without which both groups cannot coexist peacefully.

The task is far from easy, and the obstacles to the resolution of the problems between Israel and the Palestinians certainly do not simplify the matter. If we do not turn, as early as possible, to a profond self-examination of our attitudes towards the Arab minority, we will find that even if the external conflict is settled, Israel is in the throes of a painful internal struggle. The attitudes of the Jewish majority contain sufficient positive elements for building a more balanced relation with the Arab minority. What is absent so far, is a policy prepared to grapple with the essentials of the problem.

*   *   *

The Van Leer Jerusalem Foundation has chosen to deal with this issue for we believe it to be one of the three or four central problems affecting Israel's existence as a Jewish state in the coming generation. The problem is neither simple nor easy to solve. It is even conceivable that some aspects of the problem are insoluble.

The major purpose of this volume is to offer a series of articles of interest to the general public, and not only to a specific professional group.* The volume examines several aspects of

---

* There is an abundance of academic publications and specialized studies on this problem. See the excellent bibliography annotating 429 publications: Sammy Smooha and Ora Cibulski (Eds.), *Social Research on Arabs in Israel, 1948–1977, Trends and Annotated Bibliography,* Turtledove Publishing, Ramat Gan, 1978.

the problem, but does not pretend to encompass all its ramifications.

The authors of the articles reflect a wide range of personal experiences in different realms — education, academic research, literature, journalism and politics. The range of experience is necessarily reflected in different modes of expression.

The articles reflect the views of their authors, and not of The Van Leer Jerusalem Foundation, which regards this issue as a matter of public concern of the first order, but as always refrains from expounding a view of its own on affairs that are ultimately subject to political decision.

THE ARABS OF ISRAEL:
A STATISTICAL PORTRAIT

AVRAHAM BURG

In the following statistical survey of the Arabs of Israel, wherever the data were available the present situation was compared with that of 1948 and that projected for 1995; in several places, comparisons with neighboring Arab countries are also presented.

The data refer to the end of the year indicated unless otherwise stated. From 1967 on, the data include the inhabitants of East Jerusalem.

Forecasts are based on three different assumptions:

Assumption	Immigration	Emigration	Net Balance
A	0	0	0
B	25,000	15,000	10,000
C	50,000	10,000	40,000

The forecast of the Central Bureau of Statistics is based on population growth without immigration/emigration movement. Although not a reasonable assumption, we have preferred it to the other two, since changes in the composition of the Arab population in Israel will stem almost exclusively from natural increase and mortality.

Population

1. Size[1]

Year	Total population	Non-Jews (number)	Non-Jews as percentage of total population
1948	872,700	156,000	17.8
1979	3,830,000	618,000	16.0
1995[2]			
Assumption A	5,040,700	1,068,800	21.6
Assumption B	5,268,000	1,068,800	20.6
Assumption C	5,954,600	1,068,800	18.3

The data show that today one out of every six Israelis is a non-Jew; in the 1990s that proportion will most likely be one out of five.

2. Average age

Year	Total	age	Jews Total	Average age	Non-Jews Total	Average age
1948	—	—	716,000	28.9	—	—
1955	1,789,100	27.1	1,590,500	27.6	198,600	20.7
1978	3,743,600	28.9	3,141,200	30.4	596,400	23.0

Main conclusion: The non-Jewish population in Israel is younger than the Jewish population: its average age is about seven years less than the Jewish population's average age.

1   Israel Government, Prime Minister's Office, Office of the Adviser for Arab Affairs, *Demographic Data*, Yitzhak Reiter, March 1980. (Henceforth: *Demographic Data*.)
2   Central Bureau of Statistics, "Forecast of Population and Households until 1995" (in Hebrew), Jerusalem, 1978. (Henceforth: *Forecast of Population*.)

3. Population by religion and age, 1978

In Numbers

Age	Non-Jews (total)	Moslems	Christians	Druze	Jews (total)
Total	596,379	463,571	85,533	47,275	3,141,174
0–14	289,785	236,943	30,240	22,602	955,158
15–29	159,217	122,302	23,977	12,938	821,551
30–44	79,047	57,850	15,228	5,969	524,297
45–64	48,119	33,043	11,030	4,046	546,313
65+	20,221	13,433	5,058	1,720	293,855

In Percentage

Age	Non-Jews (total)	Moslems	Christians	Druze	Jews (total)
Total	100.0	100.0	100.0	100.0	100.0
0–14	48.6	51.1	35.4	47.8	30.4
15–29	26.7	26.4	28.0	27.4	26.2
30–44	13.2	12.5	17.8	12.6	16.7
45–64	8.1	7.1	12.9	8.6	17.4
65+	3.4	2.9	5.9	3.6	9.3

Main conclusion: In 1978 about 75 percent of the non-Jews in Israel were less than 30 years of age; i.e., they were born as Israeli citizens, after the establishment of the state. By comparison, in 1978 about 56 percent of the Jews were less than 30 years of age.

4. Population growth (assumption A)[3]

Between 1976–1980

Population group	Population in 1976	Births	Deaths	Net increase	Population in 1980
Total	3,493,100	490,200	124,100	366,100	3,859,200
Jews	2,959,300	362,000	108,900	253,100	3,212,400

3 Source: *Demographic Data.*

Non-Jews (total)	533,800	128,200	15,200	112,900	646,700
Moslems	411,400	107,200	11,600	95,600	506,900
Christians	80,200	11,300	2,400	8,900	89,100
Druze and others	42,200	9,700	1,200	8,500	50,700

Between 1991–1995

Population group	Population in 1991	Births	Deaths	Net increase	Population in 1995
Total	4,630,900	580,200	170,400	409,800	5,040,700
Jews	3,705,000	400,800	152,000	248,800	3,953,900
Non-Jews (total)	925,900	179,400	18,400	160,900	1,086,800
Moslems	744,200	151,100	13,700	137,400	881,600
Christians	109,300	13,900	3,200	10,700	120,000
Druze and others	72,300	14,400	1,500	12,900	85,200

Main conclusion: At the beginning of the 1990s the Arab population of Israel will reach one million.

5. *Population growth of groups by percentage (Assumption A) from 1975 to 1990*

   Jews: 25.2 percent
   Non-Jews: 73.4 percent

6. *Religious groups as percentage of non-Jewish population*

Year	Moslems	Christians	Druze
1949	67.9	21.2	9.1
1978	77.8	14.4	7.8
1980	81.1	11.0	7.9

Main conclusion: As a consequences of differences in rate of natural increase, the proportion of the different religious groups within the non-Jewish population changes; the proportion of Moslems is steadily rising.

Population Distribution by Regions and Type of Settlement[4]

1. Distribution of the Arab population by geographical region (end of 1978)

Region	Population
Galilee and the North (Northern Region, Haifa District)	309,300
Little Triangle (Hadera, Sharon, Petah Tikva Districts)	11,300
Northern Negev (Southern Region)	44,900
East Jerusalem (Jerusalem Region)	110,500
Ramle and Lod (Ramle District)	11,300
Jaffa (Tel Aviv Region)	9,500

2. Arabs of Israel by types of settlement (end of 1977)

Type of settlement	Population
Cities (Nazareth, Shfar'am, Haifa, Akko, Tel Aviv–Jaffa, Ramle, Lod, Jerusalem)	204,300
Urban settlements (21 settlements with a population of more than 5,500)	163,300
Large villages (30 villages with a population of 2,000–5,000)	105,300
Small villages (55 villages with a population of less than 2,000)	41,000
Bedouin (23 tribes in the Negev, 18 in the Galilee)	55,100

Main conclusion: The largest concentration of Arabs in Israel is in the Galilee, where they numbered about 300,000 in 1978. Two

4   Source: Office of the Adviser for Arab Affairs.

other large urban concentrations are in Jerusalem and in the Little Triangle, with about 100,000 in each in 1978.

Political Activity

1. Participation of non-Jews in Knesset elections, as voters and as elected representatives

Knesset	Participation as percentage of all eligible non-Jewish voters	Number of non-Jewish Knesset members
First Knesset (1949–1951)	79.3	3
Second Knesset (1951–1955)	85.5	6
Third Knesset (1955–1959)	91.0	7
Fourth Knesset (1959–1961)	88.9	7
Fifth Knesset (1961–1965)	85.6	7
Sixth Knesset (1965–1969)	87.8	7
Seventh Knesset (1969–1973)	82.0	7
Eighth Knesset (1973–1977)	80.0	4
Ninth Knesset (1977–1891)	75.0	7

Main conclusion: The Arab citizens of Israel have a high rate of participation in Knesset elections.

2. Arab voting for the Communist Party and its chief rivals (percentages)

Knesset election	Communist party	Ruling party	Mapam
First Knesset, 1949	22.2	61.3	0.2
S-cond Knesset, 1951	16.3	66.5	5.6
Third Knesset, 1955	15.6	62.4	7.3
Fourth Knesset, 1959	10.0	52.0	12.5
Fifth Knesset, 1961	22.7	50.8	11.0
Sixth Knesset, 1965	22.6	50.1	9.2
Seventh Knesset, 1969	28.9	56.9	—
Eighth Knesset, 1973	38.7	41.7	—
Ninth Knesset, 1977	50.6	27.0	—

Main conclusion: Over the last fifteen years the proportion of Arabs voting for the Communist Party has grown from about one-fifth of the Arab voters to about one-half.

Employment

1. Employment of the non-Jewish population, by economic branch (percentage)[5]

Economic Branch	1950	1978	Jews (1978)
Agriculture	50.0	12.6	5.4
Industry	10.0	18.8	24.2
Electricity	—	0.6	1.2
Construction	6.0	19.9	5.2
Commerce	—	11.7	11.9
Transportation	6.0	6.0	7.0
Finance	—	2.0	8.2
Public Services	—	18.0	30.3
Private Services	—	7.0	6.6

2. Non-Jews as percentage of all those employed, 1978

Economic branch	Total employed (thousands)	Non-Jews (thousands)	Percentage of non-Jews in branch
Agriculture	73.9	15.1	20.4
Industry	285.0	22.5	7.9
Electricity and Water	13.3	0.7	5.3
Construction	80.3	23.8	29.6
Commerce	143.4	14.0	9.8
Transportation	82.7	7.2	8.7
Finance	91.4	2.4	2.6
Public Services	349.9	21.5	6.1
Private Services	79.5	8.4	10.6
Not known	13.2	3.9	29.5
Total	1,212.6	119.5	9.8

5   Givat Haviva, Collection of Data.

Main conclusion: The percentage of Arabs in construction and agriculture is greater than their percentage in the general population. On the other hand, their proportion in the public services and other branches is considerably lower than their proportion in the population as a whole.

Education

1. Pupils in institutions of education

	Arab education		Jewish education	
	1948/49	1978/79	1948/49	1978/79
Total	11,129	169,952	129,688	1,000,605
Kindergartens	1,124	17,880	24,406	244,700
Elementary Schools	9,991	116,859	91,133	406,925
Special Schools	—	727	—	12,587
Intermediate Schools				
(Junior High Schools)	—	13,964	—	70,610
High Schools	14	17,207	7,168	58,220
Vocational High Schools	—	1,850	2,002	68,164
Agricultural High Schools	—	747	—	5,349
Teachers' Colleges	—	572	713	11,732
Other Institutions	—	146	583	14,141

2. Arab institutions of education, 1948/49 and 1978/79

	Number	
Type of institution	1948/49	1978/79
Kindergartens	10	(298)
Elementary	45	290
Special Elementary	—	16
Intermediate Schools		
(Junior High Schools)	—	43
High Schools	1	90
Vocational Schools	—	13
Agricultural Schools	—	2
Teachers' Colleges	—	2

3. Number of pupils passing matriculation examinations

	1948/49	1977/78[6]
Jewish Education	802	13,500
Arab Education	—	1,200

4. Non-Jewish students in institutions of higher learning[7]

Institution	1968/69	1978/79
Hebrew University of Jerusalem	205	500 (estimate)
University of Haifa	257	662
Ben-Gurion University (Beersheba)	5	200
Tel-Aviv University	48	—
Bar-Ilan University	51	—
The Technion	42	—

"The table ... proves that the process of academization in the Arab sector is very dynamic. The absolute and relative number of students has increased (the number of Jewish students is stable). The process is also reflected in the considerable, although unknown, number of Israeli Arab students studying abroad."[8]

5. Literacy among non-Jews aged 14 and above
In Thousands

	Year	Total	Men	Women
Literate	1961	64.9	45.8	19.1
Illiterate		69.5	21.6	47.9
Literate	1972	142.8	89.5	53.3
Illiterate		83.3	25.3	58.0

6   Provisional data, The Central Bureau of Statistics.
7   Estimates only.
8   Yehiel Harari, Data on the Arabs of Israel, 1978 (Givat Haviva, The Institute for Arab Studies, 1980).

In Percentages

Year	Total	Men	Women
1954	42.8	64.1	21.0
1961	48.3	68.0	28.5
1972	63.2	78.0	47.9

Health

1. Physicians and hospital beds in Middle Eastern countries[9]

	Number of persons per physician	Hospital beds per 100 persons
Saudi Arabia	4,220	1.2
Iran	3,040	0.9
Syria	3,062	2.1
Iraq	2,471	1
Egypt	1,520	—
Lebanon	1,330	—
Israel	500	6.9

2. Average life expectancy in Israel (1978)

Jews		Non-Jews	
Males	Females	Males	Females
71.9	75.6	69.1	72.0

9 Yehiel Harari, Data on the Arabs of Israel, 1978 (Givat Haviva, The Institute for Arab Studies, 1980).
10 Values calculated according to $1.00=IS6.00.

Economy

1. Gross National Product per country, in $US

Country	GNP (1972) (in million dollars)	GNP per capita
Algeria	6,120	430
Bahrein	150	670
Egypt	8,340	240
Iraq	3,730	370
Jordan	670	270
Israel[10]	11,099	3,498.5

2. Households by net income deciles, 1975/76, by percent

	Total	1	2	3	4	5	6	7	8	9	10
Jews	95.9	82.5	90.6	94.4	98.2	96.4	97.9	99.6	100	99.7	100
Non-Jews	4.1	17.5	9.4	5.6	1.8	3.6	2.1	0.4	—	0.3	—

Sources

1. Israel Central Bureau of Statistics, *Israel Statistical Abstract 1979*, no. 30.
2. Israel Central Bureau of Statistics, *Israel Statistical Abstract 1949*, no. 1, The Government Printer.
3. The Prime Minister's Office, Office of the Adviser for Arab Affairs, "Lists of non-Jewish and mixed settlements."
4. Shmuel Ne'eman Institute, *The Implications of Peace for the State of Israel*, The Technion, Zichron Yaakov, January 1979.

Chapter II

TO BE AN ARAB IN A JEWISH STATE:
PERSONAL TESTIMONIES

DIARY

ANTON SHAMMAS

For a number of reasons I have chosen to give this talk the title of Diary. In the first place, I cannot maintain, at least in a fairly well-defined early stage, that the Jewish majority regards me as it regards someone like myself who has never left his childhood home, in my case, the village of Fassuta in the north. I cannot maintain this, because in 1968, at the age of 18, I chose what I had no choice but to choose, namely to regard Hebrew as my stepmother tongue. Sometimes I feel that this was an act of cultural trespass, and that the day may come when I shall have to account for it. Sometimes, when I think about the things I see and hear and read. But I have few complaints to make in this area. One who has chosen to live in a minor key with home, a little love, a few friends and many books, is sure to have few complaints.

I know the attitude of the Jewish majority towards the Arab minority in my inner experience. It is part of my inner map. I am more familiar with the interrelation between the two cultures than with the one between the two peoples. Thus I view it with greater severity than would appear. The daily manifestations of this reality, of the relations of majority and minority, seem much more severe from where I stand. For example, the war for the lands of the Galilee — to call things by their rightful name — seems to me much less significant than the words said, and later denied, by the Chief of the Northern Command about the Arabs of the Galilee. (That the Arabs of the Galilee are "a cancer in the heart of the nation" — Ed.) It is less significant because realities are ephemeral and subject to change, but the damage done by words cannot be undone by words. A declaration broadcast by the communications media may be denied, explained away, or endowed with the ambivalence of words. This dubiousness seems to me to be much worse than any external reality.

A "diary," therefore, which relies largely on memory, the memory of words and pictures, is ruthless. It is ruthless because it is selective, and it is selective because the other alternative, which is still more ruthless, leaves but a single solution, which I dare not refer to by a single word. To circumvent this burden of memory I would at this point quote a poem by David Avidan, which was not written with reference to the subject before us. On second thought, I would use these words as a motto for the subject:

> That which above all justifies
> the loneliness, the vast despair,
> the strange bearing of the burden
> of the great loneliness and despair,
> is the plain incisive fact
> that we have nowhere else to go.

And if I may add yet another word to this lengthy preamble, it would be to warn the reader of this "diary" against coming to the hasty conclusion that it is always possible to start everything all over again, *ex nihilo.* Yet it may be best, if we really wish to continue living together in this country, to turn over a new leaf, and not only because "we have nowhere else to go." For the very fact that I stand here before you, speaking in my stepmother tongue, means that this "diary," besides recalling the forgotten, suggests that despite everything, and taking it into consideration,

it is still possible to review our route once more. I have already
stated that this is all on a personal level. I make no claim to
represent anyone but myself.

I was born in the village of Fassuta in the Galilee in 1950.
The last time this village was mentioned in the media was, I
believe, in December 1979, in a television report. "Our cor-
respondent, Gil Sadan," said the announcer, "was present during
an encounter between a paratroop unit and the villagers of
Fassuta." This encounter took place as part of a series of educational courses on the Galilee, conducted by the Israel Armed
Forces. The main point of the report was a statement that the
education of the younger generation of Jews in Israel concerning the Arabs of the Galilee is inadequate. But I, who was born
in that village, and who know the people who appeared in the
TV report, could not accept that message, and concluded with
a watchword of my own. A military unit visiting an Arab village,
with the cooperation of the chief of the local council, is hardly
a common occurrence, and certainly not for the local woman
who appeared in the report and supplied the "special color,"
the local folklore element. The soldiers entered what the cor-
respondent called, "a home bakery of Arab bread," and after
tasting "a warm *pitta* dunked in pure olive oil," it was time for
some straight questions. The first one, as broadcast, was: "What
was the general feeling here during the war?" The answer, of
course, was hesitant, evasive and ambivalent. Later the soldier,
having eaten his *pitta* in olive oil, said: "There were cameras ...
I had the feeling that they think otherwise. I'm sure they think
otherwise." I watched that report again later, in the television
studios, and I admit that the second viewing somewhat softened
the impression I had received the night that it was broadcast.
But that other man, the one like myself who never left the
village of his childhood, never had a chance to view the report
once again, and to try to understand the *educational* nature of
this educational series of the Armed Forces. And I must admit
that, with the sort of education I have had, the entire encounter

struck me as quite bizarre, to put it mildly. That "straight question" coming after the warm *pitta* in olive oil — "What was the general feeling here during the war?"....! The episode served me as a first-rate starting point for this talk, which may be an answer of sorts to the question that was not asked, namely: *"Other than during the war,* what has been the general feeling here?"

You say "pure olive oil" and my entire childhood appears before me. The old oil-press, the smoky lamp, the oil flowing from the spout into the well. And my father's hands on the lever that moves the press. This picture grew dim in the late 1950s, when the old oil-press gave way to the new electrical one in the nearby village of Hourfesh. I recall one visit to Hourfesh, in the olive harvest season, when the van that was to pick us up at two o'clock failed to arrive, and turned up at midnight, because a woman in my village had broken a leg and had to be rushed to the hospital in Nahariya in the same van, which was, I believe, the only motor vehicle in our village. Once I travelled with my father in that van, with the same driver, to Maona, to obtain a permit to go to Haifa. This was in the old days, in the time of the Military Government. Of course, in those days I did not understand the meaning of Military Government, and it was a thrill for me to go with my father all the way to Maona. Today, I would add in parenthesis, I don't care for distances or for travel, but I would not lay this at the door of the Military Government. But that is another story.

At that time my father was the village cobbler, having been the village barber during the thirties. A man of extremes, heads and feet. In a sense I seem to be following him — returning, as it were, to the head. The extremes were evident in his shop, too. On the glass pane of the cupboard he had pasted a huge portrait of Ben-Gurion, and facing it my brother, in his own work-corner, had hung a portrait of Fidel Castro. This was at the end of the fifties, when nobody in the village was reading *Ha'aretz,* much less my father, who was then teaching himself

Hebrew with the aid of books decorated with pictures of water-towers and ploughed furrows in perspective. Now I ask myself a hypothetical question: would my father have taken down the picture of Ben-Gurion, whom he called Ben-Ghorion, if he had read in *Ha'aretz*, on April 30, 1958, the following news item:

> Ben-Gurion refused to accept an identity card, because it was also printed in Arabic .... A statement by the Ministry of the Interior says that the new identity cards have been printed in both Arabic and Hebrew in conformity with the previous cards ....

Would he have taken down the picture? I don't know. Perhaps he would have dismissed the entire matter with a shrug and said: "Don't believe everything you read in the papers." I bring up this imaginary shrug because it leads me to the next item, which was later denied in a very vague way, only in reference to specific details of the picture. And the picture is this: on October 23, 1979, the evening paper *Yediot Aharonot* published the following excerpt from the already-censored portions of Yitzhak Rabin's memoirs, *Pinkas Sherut*:

> We had to deal with a very complex problem, which we had no experience in solving, namely, the fate of the civilian population of Lod and Ramlah, amounting to 50,000. Even Ben-Gurion could not suggest a solution. During the discussion at the operational headquarters he kept silent, as he always did in such situations .... We went outside and Ben-Gurion joined us. Allon asked again: "What shall we do with this population?" *Ben-Gurion raised his hand with a gesture that said, "Throw them out!"* (My emphasis, A.S.)

The rest, of course, is history.

The last time I thought about that odd couple, Ben-Gurion and my father, was on May 2, 1979, which was Independence Day. I remembered Ben-Gurion who said in one of his noblest, and least quoted, statements: "The State of Israel will maintain complete political and social equality for all its citizens, regardless of religion, race or sex." Even in his outward appearance Ben-Gurion always reminded me of my father. And I believe that my father, who was a simple cobbler, greatly admired that leader. I wonder what they would have thought about the following story.

At the end of that month of May, last year, I moved back to Jerusalem after living for ten months in Beit Jallah. During that time I had learned a good deal about myself and about the "green line" that passes through me. Mornings I travelled into town in taxis from Hebron, and evenings I went back on the Kiryat Arba bus. I saw many things that the most indulgent editor inside me would promptly excise out of this "diary."

It was on May 2, 1979, Independence Day — not an occasion of celebration for me, I regret to say — I was on my way to Tel-Aviv. When we reached the army barrier at Rachel's Tomb I saw a young soldier directing traffic with a pair of red plastic sandals in his hands. And I, a cobbler's son, sat inside the taxi and felt insulted, outraged. I don't know what the other passengers felt, but it was possible, from the comments that I overheard, in that singular moment of sight and sense, to comprehend what the occupation meant to them. I don't know if the soldier would have dared behave that way at the gates of Tel-Aviv, but I do know this: if I had to retell this story poetically, I would have chosen something Yehuda Amihai once wrote, in an entirely different context:

> Flag, severing touch with reality, flies off.
> Store-front adorned with frocks bright in blue-white.
> And all in three languages: Arabic, Hebrew and death.

Now I wonder why I should have been surprised by that soldier in the report on Fassuta who, having tasted the olive oil, asked me how I felt during the war. But to return to the present story, when I said something to another soldier at the barrier about his comrade's behavior, he answered: "Don't worry, he does it to *our* vehicles too." But I did worry, to put it mildly. Even the phrase "our vehicles" struck me at that moment as quite imprecise.

In connection with the three languages, Arabic, Hebrew and death, I am reminded of something said by Rabbi Levinger in an interview in *Ha'aretz*: "What the Arab cares about is the house and the carpet." He doesn't know how true that is. The house I grew up in had no carpet. I don't know many Arab houses that are carpeted. I greatly miss the contact with the cool concrete floor. That contact between the shoes, or the bare feet, and the *concrete* floor is something I would have difficulty in explaining to Rabbi Levinger. Today I walk on carpets, and I know how much easier it is to pull the rug out from under my feet than the ground itself. I miss the ground. My generation has come a long way from the floor to the carpet, but it remains aware of the change that has taken place — feet-inside-shoes-on-carpet-on-floor. The order is being increasingly disrupted, as for example, by red plastic slippers on the hands. The scent of leather in my father's shop is with me to this day, and plastic is a pallid and offensive substitute for that intoxicating fragrance. The red color reminds me that in this cruel bullfight between the two cultures I am the ill-fated bull. Have I carried the simile too far? I don't think so; perhaps it is a little over-simplified, but it sums things up.

In his *Birth of Tragedy* Nietzsche proposed the thesis of the eternal struggle between the Apollonian and Dionysian elements. The first, representing perfect order, control and restraint, opposes the latter, which is the spontaneous, natural, primeval element. Every cultural creation is, in the final analysis, a triumph of the Apollonian, an introduction of order into chaos, an imposition of law upon anarchy. This is the meaning of a bullfight, in which stylized motions of the matador impose themselves ultimately on the bull's fate. This is, schematically speaking, the meaning of our *corrida*, with the difference that no one

knows which role he is supposed to play. The roles change, and
the rules of the game are lost. This war between the two cultures,
the Jewish and the Arabic, is becoming increasingly like a
corrida, and many throats, on either side, are hoarse from yelling
"Olé! Olé!"

Members of my generation, who were born and received their
education in Israel, understand that expression of Rabbi Levinger's quite profoundly. The house that he talks about is "sever-
ing touch with reality." Today those fine walls, painted with
whitewash tinted with laundry blue, are the background for a
kitsch culture, or, in other words, "Arab taste." When I say
"Arab taste" in Hebrew it sounds terrible: plastic flowers and
a print with a blue lake in the sunset. The sudden exposure to
another culture upset the inner balance and placed Arab taste
in the camp of *kitsch*. For what, after all, is *kitsch*? It is a warm
pitta with olive oil on a formica-topped table under the blue
lake in the sunset. Whatever is out of its place and no longer
performs its function is *kitsch*. It wouldn't be so bad if the
kitsch were confined to the walls, but it is not. It has spread into
the local councils of the Arab villages, and even sits in the
Knesset. *Kitsch* culture is taking over Jews and Arabs alike. It is
not my intention here to discuss the phenomenon of *kitsch* in
Israeli politics, society and culture. What I am saying is that the
policy of the Israeli authorities and all their institutions is based
primarily on *kitsch*.

The official policy of the Government of Israel towards the
Arabs of Israel has always been improvised. The Prime Minister's
advisor on Arab affairs endowed the term "Arab dignitaries"
with great significance. The notion of dignity, used in a variety
of ways, has played an important part in the policy, such as it
was. An "Arab dignitary," in his natural habitat, is a patriarchal
figure, but when elected to the Knesset it becomes another matter
entirely. It would not have been easy, before the various elections,
to discover where all these dignitaries had sprung from, and
what, indeed, they had been dignified for or about.

I cannot remember the exact date, but it happened at the end
of the nineteen-fifties. I was playing in the inner courtyard of
our house, while my uncle's wife sat in the corner nearest the
street and sorted lentils. A neighbor passed by the gate, riding
on a donkey and carrying an axe, on his way to cut wood, and
without stopping greeted my uncle's wife, adding: "The *jama'a*
will be at your place soon!" My uncle's wife, who had failed
to hear his last words, asked me what he had said. I repeated
that the *jama'a* were on their way to us. Did she know who the
jama'a in question were, I asked. She answered me irritably that
since the neighbor had not deigned to stop his donkey, she could
not find out what he meant. A moment later the *jama'a* arrived,
preceded, as was the custom, by one of the village dignitaries
whose business it was to run ahead and inform the chosen hosts
who these particular *jama'a* were. On this occasion, it turned
out, it was a candidate for the Knesset, representing one of the
Arab parties allied to Mapai, and who, surrounded by sundry
dignitaries, was about to hold an impromptu meeting. I was dis-
patched to the nearby grocery to buy a box of chocolates in
honor of the visitors, and if possible find my uncle and announce
the news to him. Nowadays when I think about that event I
wish the bowl of lentils had fallen from the hands of my uncle's
wife, who had been caught out in such an undignified chore.

But that neighbor really was on his way to hew wood. I have
not invented this detail, although it is one of the most important
in the story. I don't know if Uri Loubrani was a good Advisor
on Arab Affairs, but what is chiefly remembered of his term in
office, was a statement of his that appeared in *Ha'aretz* on
April 4, 1961. Incidentally, the story about Ben-Gurion and
the identity card appeared in that newspaper in the month of
April three years before, which reminds me of the opening of
T.S. Eliot's *The Waste Land* — "April is the cruellest month . . ."
Here is what Uri Loubrani said in the one quote left from his
years in office: "It might have been better if there were no Arab
university students. If they had remained hewers of wood it

might have been easier to control them." As to control I can't
say, but certainly if they had all remained hewers of wood it is
doubtful if they would have heard of one T.S. Eliot or quoted
one of the great poems of the twentieth century. As I said before,
that which is done with words may not be undone by them.

And then, the story goes, after the hewer of wood it was the
turn of the dignitaries to arrive.

On September 16, 1979, Shmuel Toledano M.K. published an
article in *Yediot Aharonot* under the heading, "As early as 1973
a secret report was presented to Golda Meir on the nationalist
awakening among Israel's Arabs." That report was submitted on
March 8, 1973. Now that that report, or considerable portions
thereof, have been published, I should like to draw your attention
to another report, this one submitted by Mr. Toledano to the
political committee of the Alignment on April 16 (!), 1973. It
was entitled "Israeli Arabs — Policy." In the opening section we
encounter our old friend the Arab dignitary after his day was
done:

> Arab society in Israel has no leaders in the accepted sense
> of the word. The front rank of those who are in prominent
> political, religious and local office is made up almost ex-
> clusively of veteran dignitaries .... These personages gen-
> erally lack the qualities of leadership demanded by the
> younger generation of Arabs who are now seeking to take
> their place ....

But the real kernel of the report lies in its fifth chapter,
entitled, "The Principle of Reward and Punishment":

> In the effort to minimize the influence of extremist hostile
> elements among the Arabs of Israel, given the complex
> problems of this minority, a policy of Reward and Punish-
> ment has been applied in the following ways:
> 1. Personal benefits are given to positive elements and
> denied to the negative ones;

2. Certain leaders, at various levels, are encouraged by the transmission of personal benefits *through their mediation;*

3. Preferential treatment is given to certain communities, such as the Druze, the Circassians and Christians, or certain positive villages, to promote their economic and social development, in direct ratio to their integration within the State;

4. Negative groups and individuals are punished by denying them benefits. This policy has the advantage of pointing out to the Arabs of Israel, as a whole and as individuals, the advantages of integrating and the risks entailed in supporting hostile elements . . .;

5. The implementation of this policy encounters two major difficulties: (a) The democratic structure of the State does not permit efficient implementation of the policy without exposure to judicial or public reaction; (b) The difficulty of determining the application of the term "negative," mainly with regard to local councils. Thus far we have considered as negative any council dependent on the Communists, even when the majority of the council members were associated with positive parties. Thus a village might be hurt even if most of its voters supported positive political parties; (c) The difficulty of ensuring the even application of the policy of Reward and Punishment by all government and public institutions.

Outlines of Policy

1. The policy of Punishment will be intensified with regard to negative persons and groups.

2. The policy of Reward will be intensified with regard to positive persons and groups.

3. The term "negative" will be reevaluated, with the aim of reducing the category, especially with regard to local councils.

4. The Central Security Committee will determine the categories of negative and positive.

Proposed Line of Action
1. All government departments *will be required* by special order to implement the policy as determined by the Central Security Committee, or by the Interdepartmental Committee on Israeli Arabs, according to their respective functions.
2. Public institutions will be guided in the application of this policy as required.
3. A restricted internal committee will study ways and means of increasing the effectivity of the policy of reward.

(Emphases in the original, A.S.)

The above needs no comment. Nevertheless, I should like to refer to it with the concern that it deserves, and should like to point out some aspects of this report.

This text was produced in 1973, i.e., when the Alignment was in office. It is based entirely on the principle of the conditioned reflex: "Positive — you're in; negative — you're out." It is supervised by The Central Security Committee, whose very existence comes as a surprise. And I should like to ask, here and now, what may appear rather a naïve question: If the attitude towards the Arabs of Israel has been fixed along the gun-sights of that committee, why then was my generation deluded into imagining that we were to be the bridge to coexistence, not only within the boundaries of the "green line," but in the region as a whole? If I may paraphrase a trite saying — is it not true that bridges, by their very nature, are fated to be the first to burn in war and in peacetime?

But this is a rhetorical question. More directly, I would say that while I am not always familiar with the manner in which Israel's other policies were conducted, with reference to Israel's Arabs it is plain that the policy was always one of improvisation.

The very title of that chapter in the report, "The Policy of Reward and Punishment," puts my back up. That god-like tone gives me the shivers. And I don't know if the Almighty is so very pleased with the whole thing. After all, surely Mr. Toledano is wise enough to learn from the mistakes of others, much less those of the Almighty Himself — for if He apparently did not do so well with this policy of reward and punishment, it is unlikely that a mere mortal will succeed. Here again is political *kitsch* at its best: the application of religious concepts to an area as problematic and sensitive as the policy towards the Arabs of Israel.

Those two words, "negative" and "positive," are also heavily charged with military connotations. It is a paradoxical fact that Israeli army jargon, which is largely based on spoken Arabic, has done much to deepen the gulf between Arabs and Jews. While this is not the place to discuss the sorry condition of Israeli culture in general, I should like to point out one of its graver manifestations.

It is widely known that the name Kafr Kassem stands for the darkest event in the collective memory of the Arabs of Israel since the establishment of the State. It cast a very heavy shadow on the relations between Jews and Arabs in Israel. When you study the verdict given in the subsequent trial you discover the chilling fact that the fate of forty-nine inhabitants of the village of Kafr Kassem was decided with a spoken-Arabic expression *"Allah Yerahmo,"* meaning, "of blessed memory." This was the phrase used by Colonel Issachar Shadmi in his orders to the Border Guard platoon under his command. It was, of course, open to interpretation. As we know, Shadmi, unlike the other accused in that grim affair, was tried by a court-martial whose judges were appointed by the Chief of Staff, was found guilty of a technical misdemeanor, sentenced to be reprimanded and fined one *agora*. In those days the *agora* was still worth something. If that sounds cynical, consider please the abysmal cynicism of that phrase, *"Allah Yerahmo."* Now the Kafr Kassem affair must be listed as one of the things we ought to forget, while remembering, again and again, the moral we have noted before — that which was done by words cannot be undone by them. Words ought to be used precisely, especially when it is a matter of life and death — and the attitude of the Jewish majority towards the minority is a matter of life and death.

But to return to the terms "negative" and "positive." T.S. Eliot wrote, "Only those who have personality and emotions know what it means to want to escape from these things."

"Positive," in this connection, is an Arab dignitary lacking personality and emotions, barely able to spell his own name, whom I am expected to vote into the Knesset, or find myself classified as a negative and destructive element. The policy of Mapai, and later the Alignment, was devised, at least in the field of education, to attenuate the Arab personality, and then to demand that it integrate into the system of the state. The integration is carried out in the well-established tradition of "Arab taste." The Arab home is the perfect monument to this integration — tiny cups of thick black coffee on a plastic tray. This, if we may once again return to T.S. Eliot, is the "objective correlative." Which brings us back to Rabbi Levinger's statement about the "house and the carpet."

The Arab house has not only lost its original inner space, which was based on the harmonious tension of the arch stones, it has also lost its outer space. "Building without permit" has become synonymous with Arab building. However, since I am not too familiar with the approved or unapproved outline plans for the Arab villages, let me discuss the cultural outline plan of Israel's Arabs as reflected in their literature.

Until 1967, the Arabs of Israel were living under a veritable cultural quarantine. On the one hand, they were cut off from contemporary Arab culture, in all its manifestations. On the other, their understandable reservation about the Hebrew language meant that they were cut off from the world's culture, not to mention the emergent Hebrew one. Towards the end of the 1960s the poet Michel Haddad of Nazareth penned the following line, which has become the best known in local Arabic literature: "Farewell to thee, ability to breathe!" This sense of isolation within a very narrowly confined area caused Arabic literature in Israel to retreat into the safe literary haven of neo-classical formalism. In this context, what Michel Haddad was doing was a kind of building without permit. Only after 1967, when through the bookshops in the West Bank Arabic literature in Israel became exposed to influences from the Arab world, was this poet "liberated" together with the territories. But this liberation was of no avail — his image as a builder without permit has clung to him to this day. Nowadays to write in Arabic in Israel is a very lonely undertaking, and a courageous one. It is lonely because the infrastructure is missing. The outline plan is blurred and the writers cannot come home again. The traditional house has given way to the modern villa, wherein everything is counterfeit. The walls are no longer built of stone — they are, at best, surfaced with it. The village society which remained in the country after the establishment of the State has not yet lost the sense of isolation. For twenty years the Arabs of Israel breathed with one lung, and the sudden exposure to contemporary Arab culture, which took place following the 1967 war, only intensified the feeling of suffocation. Under the circumstances, Arabic literature in Israel appears miraculous, impossible. The system of Arab education in Israel, at least in my time, produced tongueless people, more at home with 7th-century Arab poetry than with that of the 20th century. These are people without a cultural past and without a future. There is only a makeshift present and an attenuated personality. The tongue has been cut out, like that of the old Arab in A.B. Yehoshua's "Facing the Forests."

The view from the window of my childhood home in the village is changing. One of these days an "observation post" will be planted on the horizon, unfamiliar and menacing. Yehoshua's student will gaze down on the tongueless old Arab. No one will let that old man speak in his own language, and in the end he will, as in the story, speak with fire. The fire that threatens

us all. Only the tongueless speak such an extreme language
— with the silent consent, if not active support, of that student.
In the meantime, the fire is still a literary solution, and the little
girl in the story does not understand what it means. I hope that
reality does imitate art, and that the student will save the child
from the fire, as he does in the story.

I meant to conclude the "diary" here, on a last chord which
strikes me as an effective summary. But I should like to add a
kind of appendix.

I said at the beginning that besides recalling the forgotten, this
"diary" suggests that despite everything, and taking it into consideration, it is still possible to reconsider our path once more,
if only because "we have nowhere else to go." I wish to add
that I would not be appearing here before you if I thought that
there was no way out of the labyrinth of our relations. Nor
would I have appeared before you if my contacts with Israel
were all summed up in this "diary." But it holds some finer
pages that I have not cited here.

In August 1958, one Ahmad Hassan of the tribe of Arab al-
Wadi near Arabeh was ordered to stand under a certain carob
tree at the entrance to the village of Deir Hanna, from sunrise
to sundown every day for six months. I don't know if he com-
plied with the order, or if that carob tree still stands. But in a
way I think that man is still standing there. In the course of the
years his children went to school, where they studied the works
of Bialik, together with Naim Yehoshua (the young Arab pro-
tagonist of A.B. Yehoshua's novel "The Lover" — Ed.), who
has become something of a literary hero, and learned about the
First and the Second Temples, and on Independence Day they
were told that it was a day of celebration and that they must
take part in it.

I should like for that man to return home, so that his children
can stand in his shade, and that they should then be free to
choose whether they wish to stand under a tree, or under the
roof. I am certain that they would choose the latter.

TESTIMONY OF AN EDUCATOR
FROM HAIFA

HANA ABU-HANA

When eighth-grade pupils in one of the country's Arab schools were asked what they wanted to be when they grew up, Said replied: "I want to be a pilot."

Let us, together, try to teach Said's teacher how to clip his pupil's wings, help him find the "educational" arguments to explain to Said that his ambition is impossibly grand. Said must be taught to be a "realist"!

Said is attentive to the frequent calls on television to the youth in Israel to enlist in programs that prepare them to be pilots or naval officers or electronics engineers. If he imagines that the call is also directed to him — he too is an Israeli youngster — it must be explained to him that the Israeli suit has different sizes, depending on who is wearing it. Said is an Israeli, but — apparently — not all *that* Israeli.

Here we come up against the central question: Who is Said? Does the Arab educator have an answer to the question of his identity?

The government literature does not speak of the Arabs in Israel as a national minority. Mention is made of minorities classified on a religious basis — Christians, Moslems and others. The reply of the former prime minister, Yitzhak Rabin, to the delegation of

Arab mayors and heads of local councils was straightforward: We recognize your cultural rights, your religious rights, but we will not recognize your national rights.

Who will convince Said that he doesn't have a national identity? How will we convince him that he belongs to one minority, while Jamil, who sits next to him, speaks the same language, lives in the same neighborhood, has the same historical roots — belongs to another, and that there is nothing linking them other than a cultural tie? In the process of identity building, where does culture end?

Does Said the Moslem have a stronger tie with Moslems in Indonesia than with Jamil the Christian, who lives alongside him, speaks his language and whom he regards as belonging to his people?

I present some of the questions as they are presented by the pupil, in a very simplistic way; the reply, however, requires a thorough discussion of the question of "levels" of national identity.

If Said cannot be a pilot, and we have succeeded in convincing him to try to be a realist, we have a "picture," which, when its details are analyzed, sheds light on some aspects of the life of Arab youth today. The Arab Students' Committee at the Technion in Haifa provided me with the following facts. In 1980 there were 223 Arab students at the Technion, 130 of them in the faculty of civil engineering.* Obviously, the best talents of a scientific-technical bent reach the Technion. But once there they come face to face with the question — what can I study so that afterwards I'll be able to find a job? That's why they flock to civil engineering. But what an awful waste of talent, and what frustration after graduation — for where will all those engineers find work? Try for a moment to put yourself in the place of the Arab

---

* The others were studying architecture (6), electrical engineering (9), mechanical engineering (5), chemical engineering (1), chemistry (4), biology (4), medicine (6).

educator, and you will feel the burden of his task and the pangs of conscience he feels when performing his role.

1.   The educate young Arabs to be "realistic" means to curtail the sweep of their imagination, to cut down their ambitions, to clip their wings, and with the motto "be a realist" to distort their being. There's an education for you!

2.   The task is even more difficult when you, as an educator, are supposed to deal with the question of the pupils' identity. From those who are supposed to give you direction, you encounter an official attitude that does not answer the question, an attitude that creates difficulties and piles up obstacles but is not able to equip you with definitions. If you want to be an educator, you cannot escape answering.

The question puzzling your pupil — who is he — also confronts you, the educator, and raises another, even more basic question: What are your educational obligations to your pupils in this matter?

Generally, to be in a minority is an uncomfortable situation. If you are in the minority because of your political views, you can fight for them and perhaps one day your views will be those of the majority. But if you are in a national minority, you have to adjust to the fact of always being in the minority, and you must fight that the hedges around the minority be so limited that your belonging to a national minority will not prevent you from participating in all areas of the life of the country. There are examples of such situations in the world. But if you are part of a minority that is constantly kept on the margins, that is always looked upon with suspicion, and that is not allowed to run even the matters closest to it (for example, the Division of Arab Education and Culture in the Ministry of Education and Culture), then the feeling is a very sore one.

When the Arab educator teaches civics, he comes upon a definition of the state's character. When the State of Israel is spoken of as the country of all those who live in it, the pupil can be made to feel that he has a part in this country and can build his future in it. But when some circles come forward and stress that this country is the Jews' country and speak of the "Judaization" of the Galilee — at the expense of the Israeli Arabs — the Arab educator is pushed into a situation many times more difficult.

I have not dealt and will not deal with the material handicaps of the Arabs schools — such as the shortage of classroom space, buildings, equipment, laboratories, agricultural schools, vocational schools, etc. These shortages and shortcomings, too, are an expression of the majority's attitude to the minority.

When we form ties between Arab pupils and Jewish pupils and begin to exchange visits, we are instantly confronted with questions by the pupils. The Arab pupils insist on knowing — Why don't we have such conditions? At the same time the Jewish pupils ask: How can you stand such conditions?

I cannot deal here with all the aspects of the suffering of the members of the Arab minority, or of the conflicts and difficulties of the Arab educator. The problems are well known and much has been said and been written about them. The question is what can be done to bring about change, or at least an improvement. I tried to raise a number of questions. I'm not here to answer them. As for solutions — I would want to get them from you. As the Arab folk saying has it: If I see to it that things are good for my neighbor, they'll be good for me too.

TESTIMONY OF AN INHABITANT
OF BAQA AL-GHARBIYA

JALAL ABU-TA'AMA

In the thirty-third year of the state's existence, the Arab minority in Israel finds itself at a perplexing juncture from which many roads branch out. In past years attention was directed mainly to the national identification with the neighboring countries and to economic and social problems, but more recently it has been the peace initiative of the president of Egypt, Anwar el-Sadat that has attracted most of the Arab population's attention.

Throughout the state's existence there have been two focuses of power for Israel's Arab population. One — the State of Israel, which has left the strong imprint of a democratic society, modes of thinking and economic well-being. And the other — the Arab countries, which, after the abolition of the Military Government and after the Six-Day War, intensified the Israeli Arabs' consciousness of Arab nationality, despite the years of having been severed from the Arab world. The Yom Kippur War, in which the Arab countries surprised the Israeli army, inspired a new feeling among the Arabs of Israel, about the potential capability of the Arab countries, upsetting the delicate balance to which they had learned to adjust.

For the first time since the establishment of the state, after thirty-two years of enmity and estrangement during which the

Arabs of Israel were caught between the hammer and the anvil and lived here subject to prejudice and discrimination, the hope was born that the longed-for peace — that would encompass the other Arab countries — would lead to real and far-reaching changes in all aspects of their life. But the realization of that hope is still a long way off. The opposition to the agreement on the part of the other Arab countries, especially the oil producers, the growing recognition the PLO has been gaining in the West, and the proposal in the United Nations to proclaim the establishment of a Palestinian state — all have been more than a bit disconcerting for the Arabs of Israel.

The electoral turnabout in May 1977 came as a disappointment to the Arab man-in-the-street, because of the extreme nationalism that had been characteristic of [Begin's] Herut movement, and for fear that the state's treatment of the Arab minority might worsen. A government headed by Menachem Begin did not awaken great expectations. Whereas in the days of Alignment rule, the government tried to deal with the burning problems by means of symbolic solutions lacking real substance, the present government, from its first day in office, simply disregards the Arab population of Israel altogether. Dozens of cabinet meetings have been devoted to the peace talks with Egypt, but not even one has been devoted to the Arabs of Israel. As will be recalled, Yitzhak Rabin's government held a number of discussions on the problems of the Arabs of Israel, and also presented proposals, some of which have been implemented in the field; but the present government has chosen to disregard the issue. The appointment of Dr. Moshe Sharon as the prime minister's adviser for Arab affairs initially raised hopes among the Arab public, but when it became evident to the new adviser that no one was listening to his advice, he returned to the Hebrew University from which he had taken leave, and the post of prime minister's adviser on Arab affairs was emptied of its content as an instrument of implementation and coordination.

In the past, it is true, the signs of positive development did begin to emerge, following the abolition of the Military Government in the mid-sixties and the integration of tens of thousands of Arab youths in the Israeli economy. While that led to economic well-being and a substantial rise in the standard of living, these are no longer able to keep the pressure valves on the Arabs shut. In Arab society it is the young in particular who are in a ferment. There are 120,000 young Arabs between the ages of 17 and 35 in the country. Most of them were born in the State of Israel, have a strong Israeli sense, fluent Hebrew and a mentality different from that of their fathers; their manners and dress are Israeli and they are in a ceaseless search for outlets for the realization of their national identity. The decline in the influence of the patriarchal *hamula** and the rise in the level of education has instilled in them a sense of loss regarding their place in Israeli society.

The Arab sector is no longer all of one cloth, with the heads of the *hamulot* promising the Establishment the support of their people at election time. There are some 25,000 Arab pupils in high schools and about 4,000 students in colleges and universities in Israel and abroad. This population, plus another 2,000 university graduates and thousands of high school graduates, thirsts to be suitably and respectably integrated into Israeli society.

While in the past Arabs with education were eagerly sought by places of employment, today job opportunities for social science and humanities graduates are scarce. As a result, thousands of Arab high school graduates, unlike their Jewish counterparts, are forced by circumstances to earn their living in agriculture, building and various service jobs. The lack of initiative on the part of wealthy Arabs, the failure on the part of the government and the Histadrut and its enterprises to encourage the industrialization of the Arab village, and the fact that places of employment are not being created in the villages have all heightened the problem of the Arab younger generation.

---

* Lineage group.

Another problem is the opposition of plant owners to the hiring of educated Arabs by their enterprises, on pseudo-security grounds that have absolutely nothing to do with security. While Jewish university graduates may not find it difficult to change their occupation — they have a wide range of possibilities — in the Arab sector the problem of employment for the educated is getting steadily worse. In the coming years the educated population will double in size and their absorption in the Jewish sector, after all the employment possibilities in the Arab sector have been exhausted, will be a serious and significant test for Israel and Israeli society. In the absence of suitable places of employment in the villages, educated Arabs can today be found teaching at Bir Zeit University in Ramallah and the Al-Najah College in Nablus, and other places of employment in the territories will undoubtedly also open their gates to Israeli Arabs.

When Arabs from the territories began to work in the Israeli economy, the question was asked — what will happen in the territories in a time of recession? How will it be possible to prevent the Arabs of the territories from joining the PLO when they are out of work? The problem of Israeli Arabs ejected from the ranks of the employed has not occurred to anyone. The decline in economic activity has, however, affected hundreds of youngsters who have remained in their villages, jobless. The adoption of more drastic measures, leading to a further curtailment of economic activity, will result in the unemployment of thousands of Israeli Arabs who work in branches of the economy most vulnerable in times of recession — the building industry, restaurants, hotels, etc. There is no doubt that young Arabs who have been fired from their places of employment and others who have been having a difficult time finding jobs, have been among the contributors to the rising tide of crime in the Arab sector, which has grown a good deal in recent years. The series of instances of arson against cars in Tayiba was symptomatic of the problem of these jobless youths.

The status of municipal government has always been higher

in the Arab sector than in the Jewish population. In the absence of other public institutions, local government in the Arab village is vested with powers that are not found in the Jewish community, thereby giving it special status. The discrimination against this authority and the short shrift it receives as compared to municipal government in Jewish towns immeasurably intensifies the sense of deprivation of the village inhabitants and of their elected officials. Government per capita grants are several times smaller in the Arab sector than in the Jewish towns and do not allow the municipal authorities to create fields of activity; income is able to cover only regular operating expenses and payment of debts. The acute shortage of classrooms, laboratories, gymnasiums, youth clubs, roads, sewage, adequate water supply systems, etc. — is a direct consequence of the budgetary limitations under which the Arab municipal authorities are forced to operate.

An examination of the budgets of two municipal authorities — one Jewish, one Arab — with the same number of inhabitants, will reveal the large discrepancy between their receipts of government grants. However more efficient the municipal tax collection system will be made, however high the rate of collection — the situation of the Arab local governing authorities will not be much improved. Complaints lodged in the past about large-scale tax evasion in the Arab sector led to special collection operations by the income- and value-added-tax authorities, which resulted in the collection of hundreds of millions of Israeli pounds. It may be hoped that this will lead to an increase in the grants to the Arab local authorities and will put a stop to the slander about the meager contribution of the Arabs of Israel to the national income.

Despite the material gains the Arabs of Israel have made in the years since the state's existence — which accelerated after the Six-Day War, with the abolishment of the Military Government and the end of the period of recession in the economy — the Arabs of Israel have not attained equal status in Israeli society. The almost total absence of joint activities and projects to increase understanding in schools, youth movements, youth camps and the like, gives rise to a feeling of estrangement and the lack of a consciousness of a common life in the country. In the past there were more activities to increase understanding, but in recent years virtually nothing has been done in this important direction. While there are a number of permanent bodies undertaking joint activities — like Beit HaGefen in Haifa, Beit Kedem in Acre, Beit Hillel in Jerusalem — their activities are on a very limited scale and for the most part always with the same participants.

Much has been said about the peace with Egypt. There has been talk of reciprocal tourism between the two countries, trade relations, culture, art, the exchange of youth delegations and the like. However, much of the Jewish population gives precedence to an acquaintance with Egypt and its inhabitants over acquaintance and establishment of ties with Israeli Arabs, who have been living with them since the founding of the state. The behavior of Arab students in the universities is to a large extent an expression of their estrangement from the Jewish students, many of whom shun them and refrain from forming any social ties with them whatever. Arabs have not been able to integrate into the Zionist parties in a suitable and respectable manner. To date, the Zionist parties have not succeeded in promoting important figures who can win real support from the Arab public.

The sense of prejudice and discrimination deeply felt by the Arabs of Israel is expressed in the events marking Land Day, which falls on March 30. Several years have passed since the events of the first Land Day.* Every year since, a number of rallies are held marking this day, which provide an outlet for frustrations in all areas of life.

---

* In 1976.

In the thirty-third year of the State of Israel's existence, the Arabs of Israel note with satisfaction their progress and the well-being they have attained during the state's existence. The contribution of the Arabs of Israel to the country's economy, especially in agriculture, is very impressive. It is their hope that along with the peace with Egypt, more attention will be paid to them and that efforts will be made to integrate them into the life of the country, with greater involvement in many and additional realms, and a removal of the barriers whose time has come to be abolished.

TESTIMONY OF A DRUZE MEMBER OF THE KNESSET

ZEIDAN ATASHI

Let me begin by expressing my hope that there will be many forums like this one for fostering awareness of their common problems among the Jewish and the Arab population. My problem is twofold. I shall speak as a Druze, a member of a minority within the Arab minority, and I will speak as a Druze, a member of a minority among the Jewish majority. I will try, therefore, to deal with both aspects of the problem. I will begin with a parable that is applicable to the Druze community. It is an old Arab fable about the crow who wanted to imitate the gait of the partridge, began to try it — but did not succeed; it wanted to revert to its own gait — and wasn't able to do so. It remained stuck in the middle, neither here nor there, neither one nor the other. I think a similar situation can be seen among a fairly large part of the Druze community, and also among some of the Moslems and Christians of Israel. The parable fit them in many instances over the last thirty-three years, and that perhaps is why we see strange phenomena among the Arab population. I say strange, because we were not accustomed to such things in the past. I will go into detail later.

There is another matter I wanted to raise. It is common in democratic — or non-democratic — regimes, for the majority to try to keep the minorities apart, the better to consolidate their rule. We have read about that in political science books, and have seen it in the history of the entire Middle East. We also see it in Israel and in other countries, democratic ones at that, and there is no reason to get into a fright over it; what is necessary is to try to deal with it.

I have cause to blame the Arab population in the State of Israel, which has never yet united — not politically and not socio-politically. If we take, for example, the manufacturers' association, or that of the farmers or the vinegrowers, we see that when they are faced with a problem they come to the Knesset in a united voice (as a "lobby") and are able to get what they want. But we Arabs are lacking a lot because we have not yet been able to create unity and to come as a "lobby." That is the personal experience I gained in the last two years within the halls of parliament. I think that this period — a period of disunity among the Arabs — and its consequences will be with us for a long time to come.

I was born in 'Isfiya to a poor family and, in terms of numbers, not a large one compared to the giant *hamulas* in 'Isfiya and Daliyat al-Karmil. Despite that, I think I have succeeded in paving a way for myself, because of my belief that I am not a guest here. I live on my land, want to believe that I enjoy rights, and I want to push as much as possible. You have to be like a bulldozer, then you may be able to succeed. And so, the *hamulot* didn't play a big role in the path I chose for myself in the early sixties. Meanwhile, I personally am encountering two strange groups in my community — and now you will see where the parable of the crow and the partridge was leading.

One group goes by the name of the Druze Initiative Committee. This committee adopts a very extreme line, but in effect is swallowed up by internal Israeli political movements, which I consider undesirable both for the Arab interest and politically. The members of this group say: We don't want to serve in the army, we don't want lands to be expropriated — a legitimate wish with which I agree — and we want to observe the Ramadan fast, as was done by the Druze before Israel was established. (The community stopped observing it after the State was established.) They approached me two years ago and wanted me to join their ranks. We had a conversation in my house. What are you offering? I asked. They answered: First of all, we don't want to serve in the army. I told them that I didn't agree with that. To serve in the army is not always an obligation. For me it is a privilege. It is a privilege, because I feel that the tradition of the Druze community has shown that your land is an inseparable part of you, and your property is an inseparable part of the national land on which you are living. If you don't take part in the defense of that land, you become a hostage. On this point, then, we didn't agree. I agree with the second point, the opposition to the expropriation of lands. On the third point, about the Ramadan, I said to them: Dear friends, perhaps I will agree with you, but first I want to conduct a brief study. Give me three days, and I'll investigate. And then I traveled to the Good Fence and met some Druze from Lebanon. I went on from there and met Druze from the Golan Heights. Personally, I hadn't encountered this problem of whether or not to celebrate. In my parents' house the holiday was observed, but the Druze of Lebanon and the Druze of the Golan Heights, who are Syrians, told me that they don't celebrate it. After several days I returned and, as promised, met with representatives of the Druze Initiative Committee, and presented them with the findings of my investigation, not necessarily in order to reject their contentions; I argued as follows: Since the Druze community in Israel is an extension of the Druze community in Lebanon and Syria, and not vice versa, and since they do not celebrate Ramadan in their countries, we only celebrated it in order to identify with the Moslem majority that existed in Palestine, and there is no shame in stopping its celebration now. We have remained divided on this issue to this day.

That, as I said, is an extremist group. There is another group, which calls itself the Druze Zionist Committee. It was formed while I was abroad. When I returned, they too approached me, in order to get me to join them. I asked them: What do you want, I too, sometimes, preach in favor of Zionism. The question is whether I can be a Zionist. We disagreed on many points — not on Zionism itself, but on the fact that you are a Druze and you pretend to be a Zionist. I don't believe that. I respect Zionism, but I don't believe in your movement, Druze Zionists. In the course of conversations with many Establishment people, there were those who said to me: Zeidan, we read in the papers that there's a group of that sort and it doesn't sound right. Who said that? Jewish figures, friends of mine, said it. And incidentally, I agree with them, it isn't right. And if that is said by Jews, why do I, as a Druze, have to believe in such a movement? I can believe in a Druze group *for* Zionism. Although we met many times in order to change the group's name, they never agreed to do so. You can also be a Moslem for Zionism. Churchill, too, was in favor of Zionism.

On the one hand, when as a member of the Knesset I speak on the Arab-Israeli issue, I am fiercely attacked by the Initiative Committee. Why? Because they believe that I've been planted somewhere on behalf of Zionism and Jewry to speak as I do. On the other hand, I am attacked by the Zionist Committee, because in the Knesset I protect, or try to clarify or raise problems of Arabs. As you see, my life is difficult.

Since I was elected to the Knesset as a young Druze I learned — and a person must learn — from the mistakes of the old-timers. I will give you as an example a proverb I cited two weeks ago in a speech I delivered in the Knesset: A man can plant anything, and he himself will uproot it. But when you plant a man — he uproots you. In Arabic its meaning is much more profound. I wasn't planted, but went to the Knesset on an electoral list called the Democratic Movement for Change, may it rest in peace. Today I am proud to be in the opposition, proud to be one of a thinking, independent, intellectual group.

You may not agree with me. I belong to Shinui and we are trying to fight for principles. I said to myself: I want to be planted here. Do I want to represent the problems of the Druze — problems on a small scale — or the problems of the Arabs of Israel — on a larger scale — or the problems of the State of Israel, on a national scale? I chose the national scale, because I don't want to be a figure that represents an ethnic group in the State of Israel; because in my contact with the public, too, I am trying to break down the concept of "minority" and "majority."

I think this concept can be shattered. There are some countries where the concept "minority" no longer exists, or if it does exist, it is only theoretical. But here, we feel it in daily life. When are you a minority? You are a minority when you emigrate, when you fall back on the state's strength, when you study with welfare support. You are a minority when nothing is yours. But why do I have to feel like that? First of all, I want all of us to be called "Israelis." I respect the national home of the Jewish people. I also fight for it and defend it. I don't want to come to the conclusion that I, in my behavior toward myself and my behavior toward others, feel like a minority. I want to be part of the national entity. I deserve to be, for I am not less than anyone else. I studied in Israeli institutions, and I want to behave as such. If some say that I am "Rakah" (Communist), I will pay no attention. If some say that I am a "Zionist," I will pay no attention. I am the one who decides my line. Sometimes I also have to impose it.

I've learned in life how, at times, to impose concepts and views, and that is what I have done in the State of Israel. Imagine what it is to be an Israeli consul in the United States. I made it to that. I thought a good deal about it before I went. Druze and Moslem friends asked me: What are you going to do, you'll sink, you'll drown, they'll kill you, you don't know what you're getting yourself into. I said: You know what, to become a national figure you have to make sacrifices. I have a state, and I have to prove to the state and the nation that I too have potential no less than the Jew who lives here, and that I can make my contribution. And I went to the United States and stayed there for four years. My contribution, I think, was quite sizeable. I'm only very sorry that the experiment of the Ministry of Foreign Affairs has not yet been repeated, and no one else has yet been sent. From my experience, when you talk as a non-Jew to Americans or to the English, you are convincing. What you say rings true. That was my feeling after every meeting. I always tried in these meetings to be credible and to tell the truth to American Jews and Gentiles alike.

The State of Israel is a normal country, like all normal democratic countries. And it also has its normal problems. We are not a society where everything is rosy, we are not without problems. We have terrible problems. That is how I presented things. But I was asked by Jews: You, as a Druze-Arab-Israeli, what are you doing here? To a Jew I would say: "By your living here in the United States, you are an American, for the Americans have not declared their country a Christian country. In the United States there is no identity card with the classification Arab, Druze, Jew. An American has a card with a name and number, and that's it. You are not asked daily, just because you are a Jew, where are you going. The same should hold for me. I want you to regard me as an Arab who lives there. You, a Jew, serve in the army of the United States, in the Marines and the Air Force, and I do the same in Israel. You are loyal here and I am loyal there. Why do you ask me? You are a Jew living in the United States and there are Jews living in France. The United States doesn't distinguish between a Jew and a Puerto Rican and an Italian. I want you, the Jew, to know that I, the Arab, can be a Druze, an Arab, an Israeli, and that there is no contradiction between the three concepts, and then I'll continue to be proud of the State of Israel, of what I am doing here and what I do there."

I'll tell an interesting story about what happened to me in downtown New York one rainy night. In those days I used to give lectures quite often, especially to young people. One evening, in one of New York's not-so-pleasant neighborhoods, I gave a talk to a group of young people. The Kadoum* affair was then at its height. Following a question from the audience I criticized what had happened at Kadoum, and said to them that the State of Israel is a state of law, and I don't think that one group or another has the right to break the laws of the State of Israel: now Gush Emunim, earlier Kadoum, it goes together. I don't agree with that. I finished the lecture and then also spoke about the Arabs, that there were instances of Arabs having been driven out. The flight of the Arabs from here in 1948 doesn't make a difference. Suddenly, a Jewish religious nationalist fellow stood up and said to me: You! Who are you, an Arab, to speak against the Kadoum group? Who's asking you at all and who's asking you to criticize Kadoum? I said to him: "My dear Jewish friend, as long as you're living here in Brooklyn and I'm living in Israel, I'm the one who speaks in the name of the State of Israel. Immigrate to Israel, and then speak Zionism!"

At the same occasion, a fellow from the PLO office in New York — whose people were generally on my heels — suddenly got up and told me: "You! You're a Zionist. They bought you cheap. Sent you for a dollar. You're looking for material comfort, you're a materialist." In short, he showered me with abuse. The Arab was young, and I'm sure he was born abroad and not here. I said to him: "My friend, I am a proud Israeli Arab. Never have I been afraid of a grenade or a bullet. I stayed on my land despite everything. I wasn't faithless to it and didn't betray it, and therefore I can speak both in the name of the Arabs of Israel and in the name of Israel."

Such situations, when you find yourself in them, are not easy. They are very difficult situations. Now I am asked about the Jewish state. I want to tell you frankly, we have developed some grating concepts. I acknowledge that it is a Jewish state, but the

---

* One of the first illegal settlements was called Kadoum.

international ear does not accept a religious-national definition of a country. For me the state is the State of Israel. I have always said — for me this is the national home of the Jewish people and I fight for it, for I have no alternative! And for me, it is the State of Israel.

It has been said to me many times — here in Israel, and also when I was recently in England — that since the laws of Judaism do not apply to me and I am not forced to convert to Judaism in order to live in the State of Israel; since I can express myself freely and can criticize the government; since I can live as a Druze with a proud religion and as an Arab with a proud nationality — I can, therefore, live as a proud Israeli citizen. For me, that is the State of Israel. There is still no substitute in the form of "Israelization," but I hope that will be achieved in the course of time. Conversion and other forms of religious coercion of non-Jews do not exist in Israel. Of all the Arabs in the Knesset today, I'm the one who noticed something in the abortion law. This law was passed by the Knesset and therefore must apply to all citizens of Israel, including the Arabs. But the law is drawn from the Halakha.* I rose and said: Fellow members, I don't want this to become a precedent in Israeli legislation, that a law drawn from the Halakha is applied to Moslems and Druze. Today, as a Member of the Knesset, and for Israel's image, I don't want it to be a precedent that legislation taken from the Halakha, which I respect, will also be supposedly applicable to the Arabs. There was once a law prohibiting polygamy, but that law was not drawn from the Halakha. I don't know that I would have agreed to it then, in order to identify with my Moslem colleagues.

I will conclude with some very minor comments. Following the Six-Day War there were some — Yigal Allon was one of them — who said that we have leaders who can announce many things on the spur of the moment, which is why we are as we are. Then someone appeared and proposed the establishment of

---

* Jewish religious law.

a Druze state on the Golan Heights, that would link the Druze on the Golan Heights with the Druze in Israel and the Druze in Syria. At the time, I was working for Israeli television, which was then in its infancy. I met with Yigal Allon, on his initiative, and with several Druze figures who thought the idea brilliant. They had already distributed appointments — one would be prime minister, another would be foreign minister and that one would be minister of the interior and of religion. I said to them: "Fellows, we don't even get along among ourselves. Let the Jews continue to handle us and let's not make revolutions in the Druze community. And secondly, who assures you, Yigal Allon, that the Druze in Syria will receive you with open arms? That the Druze of Israel are loyal to the state, does not mean that the Druze of Syria will join you tomorrow. We have no vision of establishing a state. We do not have an economy. We are not an independent nation. We do not have an independent history. Therefore, let's drop this proposal. Therefore the land once again is not ours. It is land that in the meantime is run by the Israeli army authorities, and therefore I do not believe that the Druze community deserves to establish a state, for the three reasons I mentioned. I really believe that the conflicts within the Druze comunity are so deep that it wouldn't stand a chance.

Finally, I want to return to the fable about the crow and the partridge. We are divided today in a very difficult way. We Druze do not have a Druze identity, do not have an Arab identity and are divided with regard to the Israeli identity. The near future of a community in such a situation does not bode well. We've had many disappointments. We are a community that has served in the Israel Defense Forces and has given the best of its young. I am not generalizing, and I want to be very cautious, but certain circles still regard us like all the other communities which have not served in the army. I don't mean to imply that we should be given special treatment. I want all those who served in the army, including the Druze, to be equals in the State of Israel, and not that those who served and those who did not serve be in the same classification. You cannot achieve a hundred percent equality, you cannot achieve a hundred percent satisfaction. You never can. But we will always live in such a way. Regrettably, inequality exists in one form or another. It is a policy I sense both as a citizen and as a Knesset member. When I returned from abroad, that was one of my great experiences. But immediately I put my hands to my head and said — just a minute. I returned from being a consul and thought an honor guard was being prepared for me at the airport, and some twenty cars to escort me home. At long last the consul was returning after four years!

And I sat at home for three months without a job. I thought that was being done to me because I am a Druze. I checked. I went and asked a number of people, those loaned from other institutions, not Foreign Ministry people. Foreign Ministry people return from an assignment abroad and become frustrated inside the Foreign Ministry. And then I asked someone — What is happening to you? I said: Look what's happening with me. I'm going to return to the United States. To study. I've already been accepted. I've given up. I can't live this way. You treat me like a Druze. Then the Jew said: The same thing happened to me. All they sent was a man to take the suitcases from the airport. I even paid customs in full. Nobody called me. No job has been offered me. I said: Wait, in that there's equality, and I was glad.

I want to mention another experience of mine. We are witness to the fact that the political map in Israel was very distorted in terms of the non-Jews; in the Jewish sector, and most certainly in the Arab sector, it fostered a feeling of frustration and segregation. What happened here? You, Zeidan Atashi, are a Druze — therefore you have to vote for a list headed by a Druze candidate. Fine. I go and vote. You, Jalal Abu-Ta'ama, a Moslem, go vote for the list headed by a Moslem, and you Elias Hana, the Christian, must vote for a list headed by a Christian. That is the situation. I grew up with that situation. That is how the Arab generations grew up — those who today comprise the 75 percent Alouph Hareven spoke of,* those born in the State of Israel — with a feeling of political segregation. That is why those people did not work on the national level within the Knesset. And the situation was thus fed back to the Arab youth who, except in rare instances, did not find a Jew representing him or an Arab representing him. Today, and I hope in the coming months as well, I am trying to make it through this segregation; for, again, I do not see a contradiction between my being a Druze, the son of a Druze family, in terms of religion, an Arab in language and nationality, and an Israeli. I am proud of all three.

---

* See p. 3.

TESTIMONY OF A JOURNALIST AND EDUCATOR FROM THE VILLAGE JATT

MUHAMMAD WATTAD

I was asked to give testimony. Testimony contains a good deal of self-revelation, and self-revelation in public is liable to resemble a session on the psychiatrist's couch. I hope that you, the reader, will regard my remarks as a mirror in which you also see yourself and not only us, the Arabs of Israel — for we have been living together, and apart, for some thirty years. You have undoubtedly influenced the way we have been shaped — not only in terms of national conception but also as persons. And, like it or not, we have influenced and will influence how you are shaped, both as a nation and as individuals. The fact that we will continue to have an influence in large part (but only in part) answers the question — "Where is this generation headed?" For the coming generation will certainly not be cut off from what the previous generation has done. The previous generation does not only provide background scenery — it creates, shapes and points the way. The subsequent generation will proceed — to a large or to a small extent — along the way of its predecessor.

One day I walked into the "government" of my village, the local council, and overheard a telephone conversation between the secretary of the council and, I suppose, the secretary of another council, or perhaps the head of another council, asking him, what are you supposed to do in Jatt, now that the Ministry of Health has announced that the maternity department in the Baqa Health Center is going to be closed? Upon hearing the question I smiled to myself. It was a very private smile, for a private reason. From this moment on it will no longer be private. I was born in a field, in the open air, without a midwife, without a bed and without white sheets, but my seven children were born in the very same maternity hospital, in the same department that is about to be closed. The generation that came before me did not prepare maternity hospitals for us, and yet, we are alive. Perhaps not all of my brothers born in the field survived, and for sure, many died because there was no maternity hospital. But for our children, we built, together with you, a maternity ward, and children are born in beds, with white sheets, with the help of a midwife and with proper medical care. The department may be closed, or public pressure may keep it from closing. But what is certain — that will not determine our fate. Children, like adults, will remain the same. It is our assumption that when a mother changes diapers she knows that it was her son who wet them; that when she changes his sheet she knows that it was her son who wet it. But when I went to visit my son in a Jewish school, I discovered that others wet his sheets and mattress, intentionally, for no reason other than that he is an Arab. The boy is no longer the same boy, and the assumption is no longer the same assumption.

That, then, is the generation we are preparing. It is part of the coming generation. I'm not relating these things in order to arouse pity. All of us have to take pity on ourselves. The victim is not the one whose bed was wetted. The victim is, above all, the boy who did the deed, the educators responsible for his education, and the parents responsible for his upbringing. They are the primary victims. That is part of your image as it appears in the mirror. Neither can we, the Arab citizens, be cleared of all blame. We were educated on the lap of a national movement that took the path of total rejection — rejection of everything associated with you, the Jews-Zionists, and of everything that belongs to you, both ideology and implementation. Unfortunately, not enough people among us arose and said: Stop! Let us learn something from history. A national movement cannot totally negate another national movement, blindly, and seek its destruction, because by so doing it will in the first place destroy itself, that is to say — us. As a result of this conception we are, above all, the victims of ourselves. Until there be enough people who get up and say: Whoever negates Zionism *in toto*, without any distinction between its various shades, is a fascist, is mistaken and misleads, and is destructive first of all to his own people — it is doubtful that we will be able to set out on the right road. That is our image as it appears in your mirror, and it is our obligation, first of all, to find the people among us who will negate the negators. This conception ought to be mutual, but not conditional; mutual but not symmetrical, because symmetry between two communities, two movements, is inconceivable. That, in essence, is the broad framework, within which it is possible for us to breathe and live. I'd like to pause for a while over the words "unconditioned mutuality." The word "mutuality" stems from my Israeli connection, not necessarily from my national-Arab one.

I am a Palestinian Arab in terms of my national movement that takes initiative rather than one that is dragged along, a movement whose leaders are able to act not according to conditioned reflexes but on the basis of reasoned consideration based on the facts. I would like to see leaders who declare: "If Begin wants to recognize us or not, we, for our part, recognize the Jewish national movement, the right of the Jewish people's state to exist, its right to a life of its own." Such a conception would advance our people scores of years forward. It would make us better, make us right even more. I'm prepared to forego the advantages. For me it is enough that we'll be better and more right. In this sense, I have no need for any conditioning.

But beyond the broad framework, there is the narrower frame-

work of persons, of the individuals who make up groups. A
group is a very dangerous thing. I've seen and experienced that,
both among my people and among Jews. A group tends very
easily to adopt the mentality of a herd, becoming apathetic, demonstrating an inability to make independent, constructive human
judgements. It is unable to see the individual behind the definition. We have forgotten, and tend frequently to forget, that
behind the definition "Arab," there is a person. And behind
the definition "Jew" there is — I will not say also — a person
with his desires, joys and even hates. That is perfectly human and
legitimate, and we don't give enough thought to it. When we
turn a person into a number in a group, it is very easy to trample
him together with the group. And when another group, differing
in color, nationality, religion, is trampled, it is easy to trample
those on the margins, the weak, within the trampling group
itself. The day will yet come when the discussion panel will be
"two out of every three" — members of the Jewish Oriental
communities — who will relate their personal experiences and
present their personal testimonies. The audience will share their
pain and sorrow, and in those minutes may perhaps even ask
themselves: "What has happened to us?" and the next day it
will all be forgotten. As it has been said: the convoy will continue on its way. And I add: but it will not know where it is
headed.

I see the Hatiqva quarter in southern Tel-Aviv and other
places, just as I see the Arab village Umm al-Fahm. And
when I see that a Jew is a wolf to a Jew, it is hard for me
to believe that he will be something else to an Arab. And when
I examine the roots of our existence, I find that the state does
not have a constitution, and in one or another constellation of
forces the regime will be able to draw up various devious legal-
istic devices to match its needs. It is very possible that the day
is near when laws against weak groups within the majority
population will be adopted with the same ease that today legislation and regulations are enacted which are detrimental to the

Arabs. That is perhaps only a matter of time, and if any of the readers have deluded themselves that the expropriation of the property of an Arab in Umm al-Fahm or Nablus, or the disregard for the life of an Arab — as a prisoner or demonstrator, in Nablus or Umm al-Fahm — will stop at the Green Line,* he must awaken and open his eyes to what is happening today in Jewish Israeli society. In the end, corruption and injustice will attack the heart of the Jewish community itself.

What happened in Baqa in 1952 is happening today in Tel-Aviv. And what happened twelve years ago in Nablus can happen anywhere. Whoever hastens to draw a gun in Nablus and points it at a demonstrator, can do the same in Tel-Aviv. It's only a matter of time. And you, then, are the victim. We are all in the same boat, and the one up in the bow is not far from the one in the stern. That is my feeling. I am not philosophizing. I've brought you some of my innermost reflections, in order to try to show you my mirror, in order that you see and know and come to recognize yourselves, just as I try to see and recognize myself in the mirror you are for me. Look around you. What is today's motto? We know Israeli society since the fifties. Hashomer Hatzair is a truly wonderful experience, but that movement is apparently only a way station, a place to rest for a while, to enjoy the shade and the water before moving on. The naive, as it were, remain there, those who know how to "get by" continue onward.

Our youth, yours and ours, has contempt for values. That's our work, done with our own hands. We laid down patterns and norms of life, whose motto was: "get by," and at any price. To "get by" in life, to get hold of a good job, perhaps a good place in the center, maybe, to "get by" in school, to "get by" in the army, not to be hassled. "Get by!" That is the motto, the supreme value. And that is what we are about to impart to the coming generation. Where did we set the bounds? Has any-

* Israel's 1948 boundaries.

body seen fit to set any bounds, recently, when for everything done an excuse is found, and every crime has an explanation and the times' "leading lights" are ready to justify and defend all instances of corruption? There are signs of increasing chauvinism in Israeli society — both Arab and Jewish. It is called "radicalization." It is also seen from time to time in the tables of academics, whose work I value highly. There is chauvinism that approaches fascism. It wasn't born today. We can take the Druze as an example. In the materialistic atmosphere we are creating, that of an increasing remoteness from values, the atmosphere of "getting by" and of a crude pragmatism — the son of Fadl Mansour, the Druze, is prepared to give his life for the State of Israel, which says to him each morning: "You are not wanted, even though you serve in the army." Why should my son have to see himself as obligated to defend this country, if every morning and every evening we tell him that there is one division in the State of Israel — between Jews and non-Jews.

After thirty years — including twenty years of compulsory military service by the Druze in the Israeli army, among other things to let [the northern border town of] Kiryat Shmona sleep peacefully, partly thanks to the Druze soldiers guarding the border against their Druze brethren on the other side — the problems of the Druze villages in Israel are no less acute than those of all other minority vilages. Show me one Druze moshav that has been established in the State of Israel. According to the motto, the land is "national land," and not the land of those who guard it, and, of course, the Druze are not Jews. They do not belong to that certain nationality. Take the village of Peqi'in, for example: it is so tightly closed in that it is not even possible to widen the road leading into it. And that is a Druze village with a lot of IDF officers and veteran soldiers. Someone will no doubt get up and say: The problem of building also exists among us, among the Jews. True, but let's keep the differences in proportion.

I will tell you a story that began with a dispute. Two kilometers west of my village there was a small village called Jalma, next to which Kibbutz Lahavot-Haviva was established. My father had ties with an old man from that village. His name was Mahmoud Nadf. That same Nadf went to Israel's High Court of Justice, pleading against the State of Israel, because of land seizures, and I accompanied him as translator. The problem was solved and all the families of his village were able to rehabilitate themselves. But the world is also familiar with a problem called Bir'am. Kefar Bir'am is a similar case about which a "high conscienced" and "very credible" opposition figure often promised that as soon as he became prime minister, he would return its inhabitants. He is now in the prime minister's chair and where are the inhabitants of Bir'am and where is his promise? Another example of the "credibility" that can be ascribed to the shapers of Zionist implementation these days.

In 1954 I met a very dear Jew from Lahavot-Haviva. He was called Zeevshik. He has since passed away. He would come on foot to our village and what caught my attention, as a child, was the tattoo on his arm. I asked him: What? They give you a number in the kibbutz? That was the beginning of my acquaintance with the Jewish Holocaust.

I developed expectations from the Jews, not because they are the "chosen people," but because they themselves knew and know what it means to be a minority. Those expectations, unfortunately, are on the decline. Those expectations are also waning with regard to the relations between Jews and Jews. At the beginning of my remarks I said that, like it or not, we influence the shaping of each other's character. My expectations have not come totally to grief, but I also have expectations and demands from the public to which I belong, the Arab public. First of all, that they do not wait for miracles and wonders from anyone, and not for tidings from anyone. Not from Damascus and not from Beirut. If we do not help ourselves by taking the initiative so as to arrive at the greatest possible auto-emancipation, we will be ground down — we will not be like every man, but like the dust of man. It is most definitely possible to produce a constructive Arab national consciousness that is not dependent on others. It is no exaggeration to say that we can show the way for a constructive Arab national conception, especially now that Sadat, finally, has caught on to the right wave and has mounted it.

Chapter III

MINORITY AND MAJORITY:
THE PROBLEM OF INTEGRATION

ON INTEGRATION, EQUALITY
AND COEXISTENCE

ATALLAH MANSOUR

Examination of the issue of Jewish-Arab coexistence in the country and of the question of the Israeli Arabs and their integration requires examination of the value and relative operative weight of the three principal variables in this equation: the Israeli establishment, including the ruling political parties; the Israeli Arabs themselves; and the influence of outside factors on what takes place in Israel — especially the atmosphere in the neighboring Arab countries and among the Palestinians, and their attitude towards the Arab citizens of Israel.

What in fact is Israel? Is it a national, binational or post-national state? I suspect that the majority of the Jewish public in Israel would answer simply that Israel is a Jewish state. But what is the meaning of that for the Arabs in Israel? Israel today is not a Halakhic* state and does not proclaim itself to be a theocratic state of one religious faith or for one specified ethnic group. Equal rights for all citizens is still a watchword acknowledged by all, or at least by the vast majority of establishment political parties. The laws of Israel, as a rule, do not discriminate on the basis of national origin or religion (except for the Law

---

*   According to Jewish religious law.

of Return, and most ironically, the first law passed to deal with a problem created as a consequence of the peace accord with Egypt. I refer, of course, to the law abrogating the right of the Beduin, because they are Beduin and Arabs, to petition the courts in the matter of their lands. The law does not abrogate or challenge the right of the "settlers" in the Yamit district or in Eilon Moreh to turn to the courts . . .).

An historical survey of the development of the relations between the administration representing the Jewish majority and the Arab population does not provide grounds for the frequently aired contention by spokesmen of the Israeli establishment about the supposed existence of equal regard for all the citizens of the country. The bitter experience of European Jewry, especially during the days of the Nazis, plus the threats by Arab spokesmen that pierced the air around, added ideological depth and moral justification, as it were, to a human weakness quite common in many regimes throughout the world — ignoring the rights of the minority or limiting them. Nevertheless, I believe I can point to a process, albeit a slow one, of a gradual coming to terms and acceptance of the presence of the Arab minority in Israel. Even at the height of the dark days of the Military Government, the Histadrut managed to "swallow" a part of its anti-Arab, nationalist, "Hebrew labor" heritage, and in 1954 Arab workers were accepted as members of the trade union; and in 1958 the Histadrut managed to accustom itself to the basic facts of post-Yishuv life, of the move from pre-statehood to statehood — and to all the implications of its pretension to be the *general* workers' organization, by accepting Arabs as full-fledged members.

The parties of the "labor movement" have also shown the first signs of change, of cutting themselves off from the ethnic past and of moving towards activity geared to and based on all the citizens of the country. But except for the non-Zionist Maki-Rakah,* they have yet to fully come to terms with those impli-

---

* Israel Communist Party, New Communist List.

cations of their socialist or social-democratic universalist ideals having to do with the adoption of an egalitarian approach to all the citizens of the country. Of course, a uniform position should not be attributed to all those parties. Mapam has called upon Arab members to act within its framework, but without introducing full integration. To this day there is a special Arab section within Mapam. However, it should be immediately noted that Mapam's Arab department is radically different from its counterpart in the Labor Party. Mapam has Arab members and branches in centers of Arab population, which are under the supervision and guidance of the Arab department; the latter is run by a troika of two Arabs and a Jew. By contrast, the Labor Party's Arab department is run by a Jewish party official. There are only a few Arab members in the party institutions and they generally have no influence in those institutions. The establishment of branches is still no more than a promise; the same holds in the Arab department of the Histadrut. The similarity between the two departments is so absolute that both of them are headed by Jews named Cohen — Yaacov and Raanan.

Nevertheless, I maintain that any close observer of developments related to the integration of the Arab citizens in the country will have noted that the Labor Party reached the conclusion in the early seventies that Arab citizens could be accepted into its ranks — provided that those Arabs "will represent the party ... or have served in the security forces." Independent labor councils have been established in Nazareth and Shefar'am, in 'Isfiya and in the Druze village concentration in the Western Galilee, and more recently also in Tayyiba. Three Arabs entered the Histadrut's Central Committee as part of the Alignment's allocation, a sign of gratitude for massive support by Arab voters, who rescued the Alignment's majority at the last Histadrut convention. These things can lead us to believe that we are advancing, that matters are moving.

But, in this connection I must quickly note that this progress has not yet brought us meaningfully near to equality in starting points with relation to the granting of equal opportunities. To this day the Agricultural Center still refuses to deal with the Arab cooperatives — in contradiction to the decision of the Histadrut convention and the promises of the Histadrut secretary-general, Yeruham Meshel. Hevrat Haovdim* set up an "Arab section" this year, but the Histadrut enterprises seem not to know the way to Arab population centers, nor do they employ Arab workers as engineers or in management positions. In this context I must tell a classic and true story. Shmuel Toledano, when he was the prime minister's adviser on Arab affairs, tried to persuade Solel Boneh** to hire Arab engineers, stressing that it is inconceivable that a Histadrut company employing thousands of engineers cannot find work for a few Arab engineers. A Solel Boneh spokesman replied indignantly: But we employ a Circassian engineer. Tnuva*** is today as Jewish an institution as the Rabbinate. Here, pointing up how far we have in fact progressed, I recall a story that can illustrate how deep was the abyss we were in previously, in the early sixties, with regard to integration on the governmental level. David Zechariah, who ran the Arab department of the Ministry of Agriculture for many years, up until the mid-sixties, once told me that he had "discovered" Arab farmers from Peki'in who were growing tobacco and marketing it as the produce of Hosen, the nearby Jewish moshav, all in order to receive a subsidy. Why don't they get a subsidy for their product on their own? I asked. Zechariah replied that the Arabs have been farmers for generations and do not need a subsidy, but the Jews, who have come from commerce and the services, need a push in order to be made into farmers.

I was not convinced and publicized the matter. On the day after the article's publication in *Ha'aretz*, late in the evening, David Zechariah called me for a second time and told me that he had

---

*   The Histadrut holding company.
** The Histadrut-owned construction company.
*** The Histadrut-affiliated cooperative foodstuff processor and marketer.

just returned from a meeting with the minister of agriculture, Moshe Dayan, who had informed him that from now on subsidies would be given to products the country needs, without regard to the identity of the mother or father, the name, color or religious belief of the grower.

In truth, I must note that there was a time when the Arab citizens of Israel tended to be viewed, by the government too, as a separate group, alien and hostile. Every Arab individual was forced to feel this anew every day, as he waited in line before the offices of the Military Government in order to receive a travel permit to go to the doctor, to look for work or to participate in his brother's funeral. Yes, yes. I, as a member of the editorial board of *Ha'aretz*, had to have travel permits — I keep them to this day — enabling me to go to Tiberias "as far as the cemetery." In 1966 we could travel to Safed in the daylight hours only, and on the condition that we did not go up Mt. Canaan.

But, as I have said, the gloomy picture cleared up a bit in time. Whenever elections neared, the regime of travel permits was eased until they were abolished in 1966 by Israel's most liberal prime minister since its founding, the late Levi Eshkol. Together with these concessions, here and there Arab citizens were moved up into positions involving some responsibility. The first Arab Magistrate's Court judge in Israel was named in 1957 (Elias Ktili of Nazareth). The appointment of the first District Court judge waited another ten years. Only in 1967 was Muhammed Nimer el-Huwwari named District Court judge in Nazareth. Menachem Begin promised that after he gained power, in 1977, he would appoint an Arab to the Supreme Court, again after a period of ten years; but this promise was not kept.

Advisers and Assistants and Assistants to Advisers

That, apparently, is the major difference between the labor movement and the center-right-wing parties. Since the latter have come to power they have altogether ignored the existence of Arab citizens and have frozen a process that the labor parties had begun in their last years in power — especially after the Six-Day War and the inglorious collapse of the "bridge of peace" illusion they had cultivated. The labor parties instituted a regime of discrimination and paternalism with regard to the Arab citizens, but here and there also threw crumbs to the Arab public and to their own cronies. For example, when Yigal Allon was minister of education and culture, he appointed an Arab adviser for himself and named an Arab to the post of deputy director of the Arab division in the ministry. Mapam, which was the vanguard in this realm, appointed the late M.K. Abed al-Aziz Zu'abi deputy minister of health. Mapai — the Labor Party, the Alignment — appointed M.K. Jabr Muadi deputy minister of communications and M.K. Sif el-Din Zouabi deputy speaker of the Knesset. The Ministry of Commerce and Industry also took on an Arab adviser and the office of the prime minister's adviser on Arab affairs took on an Arab deputy adviser (who has since resigned). In effect, a system parallel to the government apparatus was created, which dealt with the Arab population. The mayor of Nazareth or the mukhtar of some remote village, wanting to settle some matter, found the person who would put him in contact with the cabinet minister or even with the prime minister . . . . The Histadrut also developed similar ties. Even the National Religious Party of those days behaved like a branch of the Labor Party and appointed official or quasi-official Arab affairs "advisers" in "its" ministries (welfare, interior, religious affairs).

It all added up to a kind of integration, inferior and faulty, it is true, but integration nevertheless.

The "Tumble" Towards Rakah (New Communist List)

In 1975, Shmuel Toledano, who was then the prime minister's adviser on Arab affairs, tried to encourage local Arab politicians, the heads of local councils, to organize into a forum for national public activity. That would enable them to amass power for participation in the approaching Knesset elections. Toledano's attempt was made in light of the exhaustion of the system and of the vote-getting ability of the "notables" Mapai had adopted and used since 1949 to "consolidate" the "positive" Arab forces. The attempt, however, met with a resounding defeat, in large part because of the insistence of the government leadership of the time (Yitzhak Rabin, Yigal Allon, Shimon Peres, and Shlomo Hillel) to revive what until then had looked like the shadow of a draconic monster of the past — land expropriations. The land expropriation decision in the beginning of 1976 pushed the National Committee of Heads of Arab Local Councils in the direction of cooperation with Rakah. The first elected chairman of the Committee was Mr. Hana Mois, the head of the local council of Rama, a village in the Galilee, who was later elected member of the Knesset on the list of the Democratic Front for Peace and Equality, the left-wing front in which Rakah is the principal partner. After his death, his deputy, the mayor of Shefar'am, Ibrahim Nimer Hussein, was elected to the post. In 1981, half of the members of the Committee were from the ranks of the radical wing — Rakah people and their partners in the DFPE.

The establishment's attempt to encourage and assist the growth of a new leadership did not forestall the continued collapse of Mapai's method of "positive notables," and instead of five or six Arab Knesset members in the Mapai fold, which Mapai-Ahdut Ha'avodah-Mapam had in the sixties, they now have only two — new — Knesset members, Hamad Khalayleh from Sakhnin (Labor) and Muhammad Wattad (Mapam). In the Ninth Knesset the situation was even worse, with only one Arab representative in the Alignment's Knesset faction. But in this context I owe it to myself and to the truth to note that to this day — despite everything — about half of the Arab voters in Israel still vote for Jewish-Zionist parties. There has been a process of "radicalization," of awakening, of intensified protest and heightened frustration. But in the recent elections to the Tenth Knesset, the

Arab citizens proved that despite everything — the alienation and the neglect — they are not estranged from the general mood in the country. They turned their back on "their" small party, the Democratic Front for Peace and Equality, and in a massive way opted for the preferred choice between the two large parties, the Alignment.

The Fault of the Arabs — Their Weakness

This is the place to deal with the second variable in our equation — the Arab citizens of Israel, who today number about half a million people. The objective source of their weakness, which prevents them from being a significant pressure group in the country, lies in their history and in their recent experience. They began their way in Israel on the morrow of the War of Independence as the remnants of a people and a society. Most of them were fellahin of little education — even in comparison with the people of which they were a part. Most of the villages did not have access roads or drinking-water. Schools were rare, and only in Nazareth was there a partial high school. The first class of Arab high-school graduates completed its schooling in 1952; it consisted of fifteen graduates. Today there are nine secondary-education institutions in Nazareth, with more than 600 pupils in each year's class in this city alone. Throughout the country there are close to sixty high schools and there are almost 3,000 Arab students in Israeli universities — and that is not yet enough for me. Today the Arab students in Israel amount to less than 3 percent of the total student population, whereas the number of Arabs in the population as a whole is close to 15 percent.

But I, and whoever desires the well-being of the Arab citizens — which in my view is to the benefit of the citizenry as a whole and the country's future — can take pride in the astonishing ambition manifested by the young Arab citizens of Israel, who set out to the four corners of the globe in order to study. The son of the priest in Deir Hanna is studying medicine in the

Philippines. Three sons of a teacher in Kana are studying medicine here in Jerusalem. A worker in the Public Works Department in Nazareth has five daughters in universities. The principal of a school in Haifa has nine children who are university graduates, including five doctors. A widow from Kara in the Triangle helped three of her sons leave for Italy to study medicine; a school janitress and widow in Nazareth enabled two of her children to complete their studies. Young Arabs are studying in Hawaii, Ireland, England, Sweden, Denmark, the USSR, Czechoslovakia, Italy, France, Rumania, Turkey, and there are those already packed waiting for the border to be opened so that they can go to Cairo. My village, Gush Halav, which did not produce a single high school graduate until the late forties, can now show whoever is interested a list of doctors, engineers, lawyers, sociologists, physicists, social workers, priests, teachers and other university graduates.

Especially developed villages such as Kafr Yasif, Rama and Tayyiba have done more. The signs of this cultural blossoming can be seen even in a small and "stuck in the mud" village like 'Akbara (south of the hospital in Safed), which can easily serve as a most severe indictment of the attitude of the government in Israel towards its Arab citizens. Today's residents of 'Akbara are people from the destroyed village of Qadita, who were allowed to return and live in the country thanks to the intervention of influential Jewish friends and owing to their ties with representatives of the Jewish Yishuv during the Mandate period. At first they were housed in the abandoned Arab quarter of Rosh Pinna, but after some time they were asked to move to 'Akbara. They were permitted to restore this destroyed village and a small school was built for their children. But from the early fifties to this day they have not been allowed to build houses and have been forced to live in tin shacks. They do not have an access road, and between their shacks, in an open and foul-smelling ditch, flows the sewage of Safed. The water they drink is polluted. They have no telephone, or local committee or local council.

They do not have postal or telephone services. It's as if they lived outside the country. But they live and work in the country, and on their own send their sons and daughters to distant educational institutions — and they enter universities and complete their studies. (Incidentally, the Arab student who helped place a bomb in a Hebrew University cafeteria a few years ago was a product of this setting!) From time to time the government announces its intention to solve this problem, but the villagers, who today number three times the inhabitants of Eilon Moreh, have been suffering a "frozen" situation on the banks of the sewage of Safed for thirty years.

They are not alone. Many Arab villages are still in a similar situation. Half of the 120 Arab population centers in the country have no municipal government, and in many of the villages where such an authority does exist, many elementary services are still lacking. About a quarter of the classrooms in Arab state schools are not fit to be used as such. More than a quarter of the Arab pupils — especially girl pupils from the Moslem and Druze communities — do not complete their compulsory education. The Ministry of Education — and the people in our local councils — virtually do not lift a finger to implement this law by following up the dropouts.

Moving Ahead

Arab society in Israel can hardly be said to be marking time. When I came to live in Nazareth in the summer of 1958 I found a lone small bookstore in the city, and found the following gentlemen serving as the "government" in Nazareth:

> Muhammad Khalil Saleh — director of the local branch of the National Insurance Institute
> Said Khalil — director of the labor exchange
> George Ktili — director of the branch of the Ministry of Labor

Elias Ktili — local Magistrate's Court judge
Leila Habibi — welfare office
Sammy Jeraysi — in charge of youth probation officers (today Dr. Jeraysi)
George Saad — Labor Council
Mahmoud Zuabi — Information Center
Ibrahim Shbaat — Mapam
Elias Zahr — deputy director of customs (two Jews have since held the post of director)
Nizar Nashif — district officer
Yousef Mussafi (a Jew) — Housing
David Oren in 1958 and for the last twenty years, Shimon Matan — Arab Department of the Histadrut

In December 1980 the above Arabs continue to occupy the same positions and to sit in the same chairs. The personnel changes that did occur were the Moslem kadi, the inspector of Arab education and the Ministry of Agriculture representative. The first two retired, and the third, Mr. David Zechariah, went into private business and was replaced by another Jew, Mr. Yitzhak Ben-Haim. Not a single government worker was promoted to a position higher than director of a local branch.

But Nazareth has grown since then. Today there are more than a dozen bookstores. Then there were three lawyers in the city, today there are 36. Instead of two Arab physicians, today there are about fifty. The local Rotary Club, which was the first to actively encourage post-primary education, is not alone today. In addition to the scholarship funds of Christian communities, public and family funds have also been set up. In a city which only twenty years ago had no more than about a dozen university graduates — today the number of university lecturers is greater than the number of university students in the fifties. (About twenty Arab instructors from Israel also teach at Bir Zeit University, near Ramallah.) In October 1981 the University Graduates' Association in Nazareth had 245 members, and presumably a similar number of graduates of universities in Israel and abroad has not joined the association, which in 1981 split between the advocates and opponents of accepting the leadership of the Communists. About a third withdrew, a third continued to work and to cooperate with the Communists in the Nazareth Democratic Front (which has been running the city since 1975) and a third did not attend the annual general convention where the split took place.

As for the Arabs of Israel as a whole, mention should be made of outside elements that are beginning to show an interest in encouraging higher education among them. Rakah and its sister parties, the Communist parties of Eastern Europe, grant hundreds of scholarships to students for study in the Soviet Union and the East Bloc countries. Palestinian Arabs, on the initiative and with the participation of young Arabs who have emigrated from the country, try to make amends for their emigration and to compensate their brethren holding on in the homeland by raising money for students through the Jerusalem Scholarship Fund. But the Arabs in Israel are still far from united as a community in a way that would enable them to exploit the opportunities available to them within the framework of the law and regime in Israel. Except for the Rakah newspapers (*Al-Ittihad*, *Al-Jadid*, and *Al-Gad*) and the Greek Catholic monthly *Al-Rabita*, the Arab community in Israel does not have a general organ or an independent newspaper. The Arabs in Israel do not have a political party of their own, and the Front (of Rakah, the Black Panthers and a number of Arab figures) is, among other things, another dam blocking such organization.

I am not charging Rakah with harboring malicious intentions against the Arab minority in Israel. On the contrary, I believe it is true that Rakah, and in its earlier form as Maki (Israel Communist Party), is the only Israeli party that has given a place to the Arab citizen and enabled him to exert influence in its framework. However, the fault of Rakah is that the establishment in Israel, and the Jewish public as a whole, views it as an alien body, and that keeps it from being a source of assistance to the Arab public. Furthermore, the linkage of the Arab public with this party enables opponents in the establishment to silence the Arab voice and to shut the ears of the public against the plaints of the Arab citizens.

To the best of my knowledge, many Arabs have an ambivalent attitude towards Rakah. On the one hand, they are grateful to Rakah for standing by the Arab public against the Military Government, land expropriations, and disregard for the rights of the Arab citizens by the regime when distributing the national pie. On the other hand, this public is rankled by Rakah, for it does not hesitate to employ its organizational and propaganda steamroller to put down and trample any Arab who tries to act other than in the framework of its "front." This imperious "envy" on the part of Rakah impelled it to wage a no-holds-barred war against the attempt by Sheli [the Israeli Leftist Party] to operate among the Arabs. The attempts by Arab students and Moslem circles also ran into the Rakah steamroller. "Leeches" and "ticks" are some of the names that have been pinned on Rakah's opponents. In only one instance did a political rival attempt to fight back. Attorney Jamil Shalhoub of Haifa, a former member of the Haifa municipal council, replied to a scathing verbal attack on him by suing for libel, and was awarded compensation equivalent to more than US $20,000.

But to this day Rakah has no one to truly fear among the Arab population. The attempt by the Nazareth university graduates who broke away from the Graduates' Association promises the Arabs of Israel a national alternative to Rakah, without the doctrinaire Communist label, but the "Progressive Movement" is still in its infancy. Consistently, since the establishment of the state — except for the 1959 elections — Rakah has enlarged its share of the Arab vote. (It weakened only in 1959, because of Maki's loyalty to Moscow which turned it from Abdul Nasser to Abdul Karim Kassem, the then president of Iraq.) But since then — and like the situation until then — Rakah has been going from one success to another. In the elections to the Ninth Knesset it reached its peak, when it garnered close to fifty percent of the Arab vote. In the elections to the Tenth Knesset the process was set back substantially, largely because of the polarization between the two major blocs in the country, the Likud and the Alignment. The Arab citizenry, being somewhat closer to the Alignment, gave that party an important boost that was damaging to the Democratic Front for Peace and Equality and that impaired its steadily increasing domination of the Arab sector. Actually, the votes Rakah attracts comprise most of the political vote, that which expresses a political or national consciousness, and that expressing protest and resentment. The rest for the most part vote out of personal interest or convenience. But that "rest" still encompasses about half of the Arab public, which votes for the Alignment, the National Religious Party, the Likud or other Jewish-Zionist parties. Is that difficult to understand? I don't find it so. Life and the nature of part of our society dictate it. The members of a particular *hamula* vote together for a party that promises a chance for a pardon of a *hamula* member. Others vote for a particular party in exchange for support of their candidate in the elections to the local council. Others do so for an economic interest, the granting of building permits not in accordance with plans, and the like.

An abundant source of votes is found, for example, above the towers of the mosques. Moslem religious functionaries in Israel are the only group in the country that works and does its job in return for a "grant," and do not seem worthy of normal salaries. The ministry of religion has been promising to recognize the basic right of this group, which numbers about 150 persons, for the last ten years — but no solution has been proposed.

Moslem religious functionaries — from kadis, the religious judges, to muezzins — earn their living and are put on the list to receive "grants" on the recommendation of civil servants and government representatives; that has been so ever since all the property of the community, the waqf, was expropriated and has been managed by the government. What had been the Palestinian Arabs' focus of political and economic power during the Mandate was neutralized after the establishment of the state, and the Moslem community, which comprises the vast majority of the Arabs in Israel, lacks even a loose national organization. Twenty years ago, at the beginning of the sixties, Rakah tried to form such an organization under its aegis, to function as a "popular front," but failed. A similar attempt was made two years ago — and again "put on ice." A year ago, a group of educated Arabs from Haifa began a similar attempt — but the Moslems in Israel still do not have any representation. The government appointed "trustees" for a small part of the waqf property in a number of places, but they have not had an impact on developments. The 400,000 Moslems in Israel do not have even one religious school for training religious functionaries. The first Israeli Moslems who wanted to enroll in such an institution were able to satisfy their desire only after the Six-Day War, in Nablus or in Hebron. Today, thirty such Moslem youths are waiting for an Egyptian promise to be met that would allow them to enroll in Cairo's Al Azhar University. The office of the prime minister's adviser on Arab affairs, which in effect also fulfils the function of "directorate of the Moslem waqf," gives out scholarships, and in the past did so in conjunction with the Arab Department of the Histadrut. However, the size of these scholarships and their number are not a source of pride to those who grant them — so much so, that after the scholarship distribution ceremony of last year I was unable to obtain these elementary figures. Dr. Moshe Sharon, the prime minister's adviser on Arab affairs, refused to cite the figures. "The essence is in the intentions," he explained to me, quoting an Arab proverb; as is known, there is another proverb that says that the road to Gehenna is paved with good intentions.

Because of the abundance of "good intentions" by the government and the lack of organization, because of the failings of the Moslem community's leadership, the lack of basic coordination among the various communities making up the Arab minority in Israel and the great division between the Christian communities and between them and their leaders abroad — because of all of these factors we are not even a pressure group like Agudat Yisrael. The National Committee of Heads of Arab Local Government — the most representative organization of the Arabs in Israel — has no staff and operates without even a secretary or an office. The heads of the committee have not been able to agree on an official spokesman, and when they do manage to meet, they decide, for example, to threaten a school strike in protest against the freezing of an inadequate budget item of only IS8 million to ease the space shortage in the schools. But in their abundance of political wisdom and sensitivity they set November 29 (the date of the 1947 United Nations resolution to partition Palestine) as the day for the strike; that allowed the director-general of the Ministry of the Interior, Chaim Kuberski, to present them as politicians exploiting the hardship of children for political purposes. They called off the strike for that date, and three months later again threatened to strike; that resulted in the Ministry of Education reconfirming the allocation and committing itself to a (ten-year!) program to solve the housing problem of the schools. At the end of December 1981, the Committee called a general strike in the Arab local authorities, demanding that the government ministries increase their support so as to enable them to provide at least minimal services in their communities. The Ministry of the Interior, which at one time used to meet with representatives, this time refused to do so. It announced officially that it recognized only one representative body for all local government: the Local Government Center. The directorate of the Local Government Center, following government policy, was ready to meet with the Arab representatives as members of the Center or as representatives of their specific communities, but not as members of an Arab representative body.

The External Variable

In this state of affairs — the weakness of the Arabs in Israel and the absence of powerful liberal-universal tendencies and drives on the part of the Israeli establishment — the third variable, the external one, enters and imposes its influence. The strongest external factor in this equation is, of course, that which comes from the Arab countries as a whole, especially from the pan-Arab regimes and movements, such as Nasserism in its day, and in particular from the Palestinians. The blood ties and cultural identity between the Arabs in Israel and their brethren in and outside of the refugee camps provides the natural basis for mutual solidarity. The fear of the Arabs of Israel was based precisely on this "charge," on which they were "indicted" as a security risk and "fifth column"; the optimists in Israel who saw them as a "peace bridge" relied on the very same "point" — until the Six-Day War proved both assumptions erroneous under the existing circumstances. The Arabs in Israel did not join their brothers across the border, and on the other hand were too weak and too inferior in status to awaken their brothers in the occupied territories to the point that they would want to become citizens of Israel. Even the Druze minority, which was more integrated in the life of the country, did not succeed in inducing their brethren in the Golan Heights to seek Israeli citizenship. The few activists who did so in the summer of 1981 were forced to return their Israeli identity cards in the fall of that same year. And what option was proposed to the Palestinians in the territories?... The "generous" Labor Alignment is willing "to compromise." The densely populated Nablus area may go back to Jordan, but the Jordan Valley lands owned by Nablus residents should stay in Israel.

The Likud wants all the land free for Jewish settlement, while the population may be granted autonomy to decide on building clinics and mosques.

The Israeli establishment tried to act after its failure became evident, and at that stage an Arab was made deputy minister of health and another, deputy minister of communications. Advisers were appointed, the first district judge was sworn in; but that was like a tablet of aspirin for cancer. The "bridge" did not bear up against the strain. The Palestinians in the territories might have perhaps wanted to be annexed to Israel had they found their brothers full partners, even if only junior partners, in the state and its institutions — in the government, army, foreign service, security service, courts, press. A kind of national minority in a binational or post-national state.

But if I said that the Arabs in Israel did not join their brothers in their war against Israel — an assertion the dry statistics do not challenge — despite all the talk of those in favor and those against, there is no guarantee that that situation will continue ad infinitum. There is no doubt that the growing political power of the Palestinians at the head of the PLO is received sympathetically, even with natural sympathy, by their brethren in Israel. Declarations from PLO circles about a vague readiness to compromise with Israel and to accept it in return for a Palestinian state in the territories grant considerable legitimacy to pro-PLO declarations on the part of many Israelis — Arabs and Jews.

The peace with Egypt — and the approaching peace with the Palestinians — will, I think, ultimately also serve to boost the issue of the civil rights of the Arab minority. The Egyptian journalists who came to the country on the heels of the diplomats began to make inquiries and ask questions that had to be answered. The commercial plans of a number of Jewish contractors and Moslem politicians to turn the Hassan Bek Mosque in Jaffa into a commercial market was met with just outrage, and as expected the Moslems in Israel raised an outcry. The government was forced to intervene and block the deal. The Egyptian embassy in Tel-Aviv followed the affair and expressed its satisfaction with the solution in a public announcement according to which the Egyptian government will contribute a modest sum for the restoration and furnishing of the run-down mosque. I have no doubt that a peace settlement will encourage the Arab minority to unite to fight for its rights, without the fear that security arguments will be waved before it and without fear of administrative decrees limiting movement or sanctioning arrests. In my view, the Israeli establishment, the "left" and the "right," will do well to remember in time that it is not possible to leave 15 percent of the country's population outside the pale; to bring them into participation, all the government and public institutions — including the parties — will have to cut themselves off in some measure from their tribal-communal heritage and begin to see all the citizens of the country as their potential "clients." It is inconceivable that lands in the public domain will continue to be called (Jewish) national lands. *Pitta*, too, is bread, not cake (which is not subsidized). The Arab citizens of the country are not aliens, and therefore a basic law must be enacted guaranteeing what is stated in the Declaration of Independence and forbidding a cabinet minister to call them "aliens" or to view the olive trees they plant as a "take-over of national lands." A state employee who calls for restrictions on part of the citizenry and advocates harming them must find himself an outcast banished from the system. And in general, the Ministry of Education and Culture must work out a program for Jews and Arabs that would teach them to see what they have in common; that is a supreme national interest. That can be done only when the values of the equality of all God's creatures and of all the citizens before the law are stressed, driven home and underscored. I am perfectly aware that the most common contention of the Israeli establishment and of a good part of the Jewish public is: And what about military service? To that I reply: When the Israeli leadership takes action in the direction of truly equal rights for all citizens, it will most certainly be entitled — and obligated — to demand that everyone give what follows from citizenship — including military service. But military service is not a magic solution. Even today, when there is no equality, and no attempt to promote equality is evident, Druze — who are

Arabs no less than their Christian and Moslem neighbors — serve in the framework of compulsory service, and many Beduin volunteer for combat units; nevertheless, these "army service" groups are not treated equally, not as individuals or as communities. A symbol of the failure of the present policy, as I see it, is a Druze IDF officer serving the Jewish state at the Good Fence, that same fence intended for giving aid to Christians against the Druze in Lebanon. That is not a fiction. Such a person actually exists. He lives and breathes — and attests to the absurd. And Major Sa'ad Hadad shells the "Ka'aba" of the Druze in Al-Biada, near Hazbia.

Another symbol, for those in need of additional symbols, can be found in the courtyard of the tin shacks that serve as the state school in 'Akbara. There, on Independence Day evening, on the banks of the sewage of the city of the Kabbalists, the offspring of the village Qadita will sing "So long as within our breasts the Jewish heart beats true...".

This perhaps is the place to inform the readers that I do not challenge the right of the Jews to have a state of their own, just as the French and the English have a state of their own — but the Jews' state is not entitled to ignore the rights of the minority living within its midst, either on the symbolic-emotional level or on the practical level. There is certainly room for a law that would outlaw all discrimination against citizens, and symbols must be created with which all the citizens can identify. Without these it might be possible to patch up the present threadbare policy, but I do not recommend building the house of the future on that basis — not that of my children or that of all the children of the State of Israel. Only the integration of the Arab citizens in Israel will allow Israel to become an integral part of the region and will blunt the edge of the political and emotional opposition to its existence. Only peace at home will pave the way to acceptance and conciliation with the neighbors. A "peace treaty" is signed by enemies, but the relations of peace are built on the basis of participation and integration.

APPENDIX

Arab National Representation in Israel

As has been noted, the Arab citizens of Israel are not represented in the government, the General Staff, the foreign service, the High Court of Justice or at the top levels of public and economic administration. Nevertheless, Arab citizens have made their way to a number of positions. Following is a list with names describing the situation as of December, 1981.

The Central Committee of the Histadrut (3 Arabs):
  George Saad, secretary of the Nazareth Labor Council
  Yosef Khamis, deputy chairman of the Histadrut Arab
      Department
  Nawaf Massalha, deputy chairman of the Histadrut Arab
      Department
The Tenth Knesset (5 Arab MKs, out of a total of 120):
  Toufiq Toubi (Democratic Front for Peace and Equality)
  Toufiq Ziad (DFPE)
  Amal Nassr al-Din (Likud, Herut)
  Hamad Khalayleh (Alignment, Labor)
  Muhammad Wattad (Alignment, Mapam)
Hebrew Literature
  Sabri Jiryis — publicistics
  Atallah Mansour — fiction
  Anton Shammas — poetry
  Naim 'Araydeh — poetry
Hebrew Journalism (by seniority)
  Ibrahim Shbaat (Israel News Service)
  Atallah Mansour *(Ha'aretz)*
  Anan Safadi *(Jerusalem Post)*
  Kassem Zayd *(Al Hamishmar)*
  Muhammad Wattad *(Al Hamishmar)*
  Toufiq Khouri *(Yediot Ahronot)*

Rafiq Halabi (television)

Bassam Jaber (radio)

Zohair Bahloul (radio)

Arabs have also played with first-league Israeli soccer teams, including top teams. Among them:

Rifa'at Turq (Hapoel Tel-Aviv)

Ali Othmaan (Hapoel Jerusalem)

Nabil Mansour (Hapoel Acre)

Amar Salah (Hapoel Petah Tiqva)

Shafiq al-Hozayel (Hapoel Beersheba)

Kaid Abu-Ahmed (Hapoel Upper Nazareth)

Hamzi Abu-Lil (Hapoel Lod)

Said Qazmouz (Hapoel Tiberias)

Similarly, a number of Arab boxers and weightlifters represent Israel and are national champions:

Ghanem Mahroum (boxing)

Adib Nisnas (boxing)

Ghanem Mahroum (boxing)

'Adnaan Kudrouj (weightlifting)

ISSUES IN ARAB-JEWISH RELATIONS IN ISRAEL*

SAMMY SMOOHA

The issues

There are many issues that cloud Arab-Jewish relations. These are major questions on which Jews and Arabs tend to take different stands, and which must be grappled with if the problem of Arab-Jewish coexistence is to be dealt with seriously. Following is a short inexhaustive list of issues:

1. *Ethnic Stratification.* What is the place of the Arabs in Israel's social stratification? Can they compete with Jews on an equal basis? Can they attain the same rate of social mobility as the Jews? In order to assess the socioeconomic achievements of the Arabs of Israel, with whom should they be compared, and with whom do they compare themselves (Palestinians in the occupied territories, Arabs in Arab countries, Jews in Israel, residents of Western countries, etc.)?

* This study was supported by a grant from the Institute for the Research and Development of Arab Education, University of Haifa, and a grant from the Ford Foundation received through the Israel Foundations Trustees. For a complete report of the findings, see Sammy Smooha, *The Orientation and Politicization of the Arab Minority in Israel*, The Jewish-Arab Center, University of Haifa, Haifa 1980.

2. *Cultural Hegemony.* Do the cultural differences that exist between Arabs and Jews in Israel create a situation or a feeling of Jewish cultural hegemony? What, if any, cultural changes must the Arabs of Israel undergo? Is "Western culture" or "Israeli culture" a desirable model for the Arabs of Israel? Should "Israeli culture" adopt a Middle Eastern orientation?

3. *Legitimacy of the State.* Does Israel today have a right to exist as a state, and is that right absolute or is it conditional? Does Israel have a right to exist as a Jewish-Zionist state? With what elements of the state's Jewish-Zionist character are the Arabs prepared to come to terms, and what elements do they deem it crucial to change or discard? The objectives of Zionism, the special status of Zionist institutions (the Jewish Agency and the Jewish National Fund) in the country, the Law of Return, immigration policies, the actual status of the Hebrew and Arabic languages and the homeland question (Israel as a Jewish or a common Arab-Jewish homeland) have each to be dealt with specifically.

4. *The Israeli-Arab Conflict.* What is the "solution" to the Israeli-Arab conflict envisioned by the Arabs? How much do they diverge from the Israeli national operative consensus on the conflict? The following points must be dealt with: the settlements in Judea and Samaria, the peace treaty with Egypt, the Palestinians as a nation, Israel's withdrawal to its pre–June 1967 boundaries, the redivision of Jerusalem, the establishment of a Palestinian state in the West Bank and the Gaza Strip, the PLO as the representative organization of the Palestinian people, and the granting of the right of return to refugees to Israel within the "green line" [the pre–June 1967 borders]. Should the Arabs of Israel abandon their passive stance and become a "party" to the conflict? And if so, what role should they play?

5. *Collective Identity.* Who are the Arabs in Israel — Israeli Arabs, Palestinian Arabs in Israel, Palestinian Arabs, or do they have some other identity? Do they maintain more cultural, social, economic and national ties with the Palestinians than with the Jews in Israel? Do they look for solutions to their problems within Israel or outside of Israel?

6. *Social Separation.* Should the existing separation between Arabs and Jews in settlements, neighborhoods, schools, Arab departments (in government offices, the Histadrut, and the large political parties) and other frameworks be maintained, or is integration more desirable? Should compulsory civilian service be introduced for the Arabs in place of military service? Should compulsory military service be introduced for the Arabs under certain circumstances?

7. *Institutional Autonomy.* Should the Arabs decide upon and run Arab education by themselves? What form of political organization is most suitable for the Arabs of Israel — integration in the existing Zionist parties, integration in Rakah,* a continuation of the Arab lists, the establishment of Arab parties associated with the existing parties (such as a "sister party" to the Labor Party), the formation of mixed Jewish-Arab non-Zionist parties (in addition to Rakah), the establishment of independent Arab national parties, or some other form? Should additional independent Arab organizations be formed, such as an Arab university, a trade union, a radio or television station?

8. *A Status of National Minority.* Should the Arabs in Israel be satisfied with individual civil rights or should they strive to achieve the status of a national minority having certain collective rights — such as an official national leadership recognized by the authorities, proportional representation with separate balloting

* New Communist List.

and institutional and even administrative autonomy in certain regions? On this, should a distinction be drawn between the Druze and the others?

9. *Leadership.* Do the Arabs in Israel today have a credible national leadership? This should be examined with reference to the outstanding figures in the following bodies: the Arab election lists, Rakah, the Committee of Heads of Arab Local Councils, the Committee for Defence of Arab Lands, the Druze Initiative Committee, the National Committee of Arab Students, the *Al Twat* group, the Sons of the Village Movement, the Progressive National Movement and the PLO.*

10. *Educational Goals.* What should be the goals of Arab education? Goals in three realms should be dealt with: the Arab cultural heritage, Jewish-Arab biculturalism (including bilingualism) and nationalism.

---

* Following is a brief comment on the above leadership groups.
The Arab election lists are usually headed by dignitaries and public figures affiliated to the Zionist parties. Rakah is the Israel Communist Party which is predominantly Arab in constituency and activity. The Committee of Heads of Arab Local Councils is composed of elected leaders to Arab local councils. The Committee for the Defence of Arab Lands was formed in 1975 in opposition to impending land expropriations and it called for the Land Day general strike on March 30, 1976. The Druze Initiative Committee, which is affiliated to Rakah, opposes the draft of Druzes to the army and advocates the view that Druzes are and should be treated as Arabs. The National Committee of Arab Students is a committee of all Arab university students in the country and is headed by students identified with Rakah. The Al-Twat group comprises Arab intellectuals and others dedicated to the development of Arab education and culture and particularly to the formation of an Arab University in Galilee. The Sons of the Village Movement is a rejectionist pro-PLO group in ideology active in local policymaking in a number of villages in the Little Triangle and the Galilee. The Progressive National Movement is a rejectionist group of Arab university students.

11. *Deprivation and Alienation.*   In what areas are the Arabs
deprived? What are the sources of their alienation? What is the
share of government policy in their deprivation and alienation?
Should the Arabs be included in the "preferential" policy applied in Israel to disadvantaged pupils in education, to development towns, to the rehabilitation of impoverished neighborhoods (Project Renewal) etc.?

12. *Desires for the Future.*   What future is desirable for the
Arabs in Israel — a separate but equal part in the state, part of
a Palestinian state alongside the State of Israel or part of a democratic secular state to be established on the entire territory of
Mandatory Palestine?

13. *Strategies for Change.*   Can the interests of the Arabs of
Israel be promoted by democratic means, such as propaganda,
pressure and voting in elections? Do the Arabs of Israel also
have to adopt more forceful measures, such as protests abroad,
demonstrations, general strikes and the boycott of institutions?
Under certain circumstances should they also resort to non-legal
means, such as unlicensed demonstrations or resistance by force?
What mix of political strategies is possible or desirable for improving the situation of the Arabs in the country — parliamentary
politics, extra-parliamentary politics or extra-legal politics?

14. *Orientation Types.*   How can the Arabs in Israel be classified in terms of their attitude towards the state and their readiness
to live in it as members of a minority? Are there crystalized and
consistent orientations related to the above-mentioned dilemmas
in Jewish-Arab relations? How can Arabs be distinguished
according to their orientation? Is orientation related to personal
identity? Is orientation influenced by age, education, place of
residence, religious community, exposure to the various media
(press, radio, television), contact with Jews, having had one's land
expropriated, or other factors? Is the division of the Arabs into

types of orientation indistinct in reality or does it indicate a deep
internal split (a division into camps)? Do the Arabs themselves
engage in such classification in their daily interpersonal relations?
Do Arabs of different orientation types differ in their patterns
of socialization, their organizational-political base and their
problems with Israeli society?

The 1976 Arab Survey

If we had precise knowledge of the answers given by Jews and
Arabs to all of the above questions, we could determine the extent of agreement and discord between them. An attempt in
this direction was made on the basis of a survey of a representative sample of the Arab population that was conducted in the
summer of 1976. That was the first sample survey of its kind
to be conducted in the country. Seven hundred and twenty-two
(722) Arab subjects were interviewed, comprising a representative
cross-section of the population — young and old, men and
women, Druze, Christians and Moslems, residents of the Negev,
the Triangle, the coastal strip and the Galilee, and students. A
small Jewish sample (148 subjects) was also taken for purposes
of comparison.

Major Trends

Analysis of the data of the survey shows that the Arabs are in
the midst of a process of politicization characterized by three
interrelated trends — radicalism, factionalism and incorporation.
The survey data shed light on these trends.

1. *Radicalism.* Radicalism means a deviation on the part of
the Arabs from the norms established by the Jews. In this sense,
the responses of the Jews in the survey comprise the measuring
rod for Arab radicalism. The Zionist ideology forms the unwrit-
ten constitution of the State of Israel, and the Jews in the survey

subscribed to it without qualification. In their responses, the Arabs revealed the extent of their opposition to Zionism and their reservations about it. The majority said that an Arab cannot be an equal citizen and identify with Israel as a Jewish-Zionist state. They held that the Law of Return ought to be amended or rescinded. They also thought that Zionism is a racist movement. In other words, it is clear that in the eyes of the Arabs, Israel does not have a right to exist as a Jewish-Zionist state. As for Israel's right to exist at all, 50 percent acknowledged that right without reservation, 29 percent recognized it with reservation, and 21 percent denied that right.

It is possible to generalize, on the basis of the survey findings and of Arab pronouncements, that the majority of the Arabs (a) accept Israel as a state, but (b) repudiate its Jewish-Zionist character and (c) wish to transform it into a binational state. Binationalism which the Arab majority totally dismissed before 1948 is of course the best option for them as a minority in contemporary Israel. On the other hand, the Jews continue to oppose binationalism and now, being the dominant majority, on firmer grounds than ever before.

The radicalism of the Arabs is also discernible in another cardinal area — the Israeli-Arab conflict. It can be said by way of generalization that the Arabs do not at all accept the operative Israeli consensus about the conflict. The Arabs agree among themselves — in opposition to the view of the Jews — that Israel must recognize the Palestinian people's right to self-determination, and that it must withdraw to the 1967 boundaries, recognize the PLO as the legitimate representative of the Palestinian people, allow the establishment of a Palestinian state in the West Bank and the Gaza Strip, and give the 1948 refugees the right to return to Israel within the "green line."

2. *Factionalism.* Radicalism among the Arabs exists alongside their deep internal split, and not in opposition to it. There is no agreement among the Arabs on their status as a minority in the

country or on their position vis-à-vis the state. The extent of the internal division within the Arab population can be seen by combining the two important questions mentioned above: Does Israel have a right to exist? Can an Arab be an equal citizen and identify with the state? About 20 percent of the respondents replied positively and without qualification to both questions, about 20 percent answered with an unqualified negative, and about 60 percent replied with some measure of reservation.

Closer examination indicates that this division indeed reflects a deep political split between three camps among the Arabs: the accommodating (20 percent), the reserved (60 percent) and the dissidents (20 percent). The accommodating are prepared to accept their status as a minority in the country, but demand greater opportunities for participation and equality. They have linked their fate with the Jews and act through the Zionist establishment to improve their situation. The vast majority of the reserved are prepared to live in the country as a minority, but demand that the conditions of Jewish-Arab coexistence be substantially reconstituted. These demands include a weakening of the state's Zionist character, opening up of the stratification system, enabling Arabs to participate at all levels and in all activities, a diversification of Israeli culture and its reorientation in a Middle Eastern direction, and adoption of the above-mentioned "Palestinian" solution to the Israeli-Arab conflict. The camp of the reserved identifies with the ideology and leadership of Rakah. The third camp, the dissidents, rejects the status of a minority in the State of Israel and advocates a political remapping of the region — a change that would free the Arabs from a minority status. The ideology and leadership of this camp is supplied by the PLO, and in rural areas by the Sons of the Village Movement and the Progressive National Movement.

There is deep disagreement between the three camps over most of the questions related to Jewish-Arab relations and the Arabs' status within the state.

3. *Incorporation (Israeliness)*. The third trend emerging from the study is an increasing incorporation of Arabs in Israeli society, or what can be called Israeliness. Most of the Arabs are bilingual and bicultural. They have daily contact with Jews. Their way of life is becoming Western. They are exposed to the same communications media as the Jews. They purchase the same consumer goods as the Israelis. They take the Jews as their comparison group with regard both to socioeconomic achievements and norms of behavior. They feel that their fate is tied more to Israel than to that of their brothers on the other side of the "green line." The "Palestinian" solution of the conflict, which they favor, is meant for the Palestinians and not for them. They have no intention of moving to a Palestinian state once such a state is established.

The growing internal division and Israeliness of the Arabs in Israel give their radicalism a meaning different from the usual. What we are witnessing here is not the formation of an Arab majority hostile to the state. The Arabs are a minority that differs with the dominant Jewish majority on basic questions, but it is interested in coexistence along with certain changes in its terms; what is more, the minority is itself divided on its demands from the majority. It looks for the solution of its problems within Israel, not outside of it.

Finally, the study shows that the Arabs draw an appreciable part of their radicalism from uncompromising positions, rigid attitudes and policies of the Jews. When the factors determining which Arab respondents belonged to which camp were examined, the following were found to be the most important "predictors": exposure to "Zionist" versus "non-Zionist" media, contact with Jews, having been affected by land expropriations, community status (a division between Druze, Beduin, Christians, and Moslems, reflecting the degree of being favored by the authorities) and the local services provided. All these factors allow for "intervention" by policy. By contrast, age, sex and education, which are "stychic" variables, were not found to have influence. These findings are quite encouraging, for they clearly attest that Jewish-Arab relations are in fact susceptible to intervention and change, and that better arrangements can be reached, provided there is willingness to compromise and to take the other side into consideration.

Chapter IV

THE PROBLEM OF EDUCATION

ARAB EDUCATION IN A JEWISH STATE — MAJOR DILEMMAS

SAAD SARSOUR

About half a million Arabs live in Israel today. Some of them were in the country before the state was established, and some (the majority) were born in what was already the State of Israel. This is a minority of recent creation and many of its members have not yet reconciled themselves to their minority status. They explain that by the fact that they are part of the Arab world, which is the majority in the region of the world where Israel is located.

The Arab citizens of Israel are linked by ties of kinship, religion, culture, heritage and history with the Arab nation, which today is in a state of war with Israel. The resulting situation for the Arab in Israel is thus one in which members of his people are fighting his country.

Israel is a democratic state, but it is also a Jewish-Zionist one. It is not a civic state. This feature of the State of Israel sometimes gives rise to situations characterized by contradiction.

As a consequence of these features of the State of Israel and of the minority people in the country, social problems arise having to do with majority-minority relations. In the following pages we shall try to deal with some of those problems related to the education of Arab children in the Jewish state.

The Goals of the Education of Arab Children

In paragraph 2 of the State Education Law of 1953, the State of Israel laid down one educational goal for all pupils in Israel, Jews and non-Jews alike. The object of state education was "to base elementary education in the State of Israel on the values of Jewish culture and the achievements of science, on love of the homeland and loyalty to the State and the Jewish people, on practice in agricultural work and handicraft, on *chalutzic* (pioneer) training, and on the striving for a society built on freedom, equality, tolerance, mutual assistance and love of mankind." In time it became evident that this goal was not suited to the Arab child to the same extent as it was to the Jewish child (although there have been differences of view even on this point), and that much of it could not be implemented in the Arab educational system. This goal was subjected to criticism from various directions, its critics contending that it was not suited to the Arab child in Israel at that stage, given the social and political circumstances within which he lived. They asked, for example, how it was possible to inculcate loyalty to the State of Israel and to educate the Arab child for a society based on freedom, equality and tolerance at a time when the Arab citizen was living under military rule, which by its very nature clashes with these democratic values? (The Military Government imposed on the Arab citizens of Israel for security and other reasons was abolished in 1966.) And how was it possible to demand that the Arab child be loyal to the Jewish people in the Diaspora? Was it necessary for the Arab child to receive *chalutzic* training? And what of the place of Arab culture in the education of the Arab child in Israel? And that was not all.

In the seventies, attempts were made for the first time to formulate educational goals specifically for the education of Arab children in Israel. In February 1972, the minister of education and culture approved "basic orientations for Arab education in Israel," as follows:

1. Education in the values of peace.

2. Education for loyalty to the State of Israel by stressing the common interests of all its citizens, while promoting what is distinctive about the Arabs of Israel.

3. The operation of programs designed to facilitate social and economic absorption.

4. Education of the Arab girl towards independence and improvement in her status.

These orientations were known as the "Yadlin document," after Aharon Yadlin, the then deputy minister of education (and later, minister of education) who headed the committee that formulated them.

We will not deal here with these orientations, since two years after they were approved, but before the Arab educational system had begun to gear up for their implementation, the Arab Education for the Eighties planning team began to discuss new proposals for the goals of Arab education. This team came up with its own proposal, based on the Yadlin document and on the goals of state education of 1953. Its proposal was approved by the minister of education in March 1975, and was published in 1976 in a book on the proposed plan for "Education in Israel in the Eighties" along with the other goals of education for Israel's children. In this book the goals of education appear under four headings: common goals for all pupils in Israel (Jews and non-Jews) and special goals for Jews, Arabs and Druze.

The educational goals common to all the pupils are general, universal, humanistic, democratic goals suitable for everyone. The distinctive goals try to meet both the needs of the state and the special needs of the various population groups in Israel. The educational goals specific to the Arab children, for example, permit the cultivation of the cultural distinctiveness of the Arabs of Israel and require an acquaintance with Jewish culture and loyalty to the state.

It may be supposed that the distinctive educational goals are the product of serious thought, that the differences between them are meaningful and that they are not merely words put down hastily or thoughtlessly. For that reason, examination of the distinctive goals and comparison between them — noting what is present here and absent there — should help to shed light on their nature and intent.

The following emerges from a comparison of the three distinctive goals:

1. The goal of the education of the Arab child is to gear the Arab citizen not to take part in the building of his country — the State of Israel. That emerges from the fact that while the distinctive educational goal for the Druze stresses the participation of the Druze child in the building of the country, the educational goal specific to the Arab child makes no mention of that whatever.

2. The distinctive educational goals for the Arab and Druze children speak of the Land of Israel as the common homeland of all the citizens of Israel. The educational goal specific to Jewish children ignores this and does not yet regard Israel as the homeland of all the country's citizens.

3. The distinctive educational goals for the Jews and the Druze stress the importance of cultivating the relationship between them and the members of their people elsewhere in the world. The distinctive educational goal for Arab children ignores this. This, of course, can be understood in light of the hostile relations existing between the State of Israel and the Arab peoples.

4. The distinctive educational goals for the two minority groups (Arabs and Druze) stress the importance of educating the children to aspire for peace between Israel and its neighbors. That is absent from the distinctive educational goal for the Jewish child. The erroneous impression received here is that the minority children are contentious and belligerent, while the Jewish child by nature is a pursuer of peace. Or is it that peace is more important for the minority children than for the Jewish children in the State of Israel?

Undoubtedly the setting of educational goals is in general no easy task. It is considerably more difficult when the goals are for the education of the Arab minority in a Jewish state fighting for its survival, and the minority is perceived as a security encumbrance.

Curricula

Curricula are the means by which the state seeks to attain the educational goals it has set. Accordingly, we find that the curricula in the Arab schools include Jewish and Zionist subject matter as a way of heightening the Israeliness of the Arabs of Israel. The Arab child learns about the link between the Jews in the Diaspora and the Land of Israel, the Zionist movement, immigration to the country, the revival of the Hebrew language and *chalutziut* (pioneering). The Arab high school pupil even studies the sacred writings of the Jews seven times more than his own scripture. (Peres et al., 1968); in the matriculation examinations he is tested on chapters from the Jewish Bible but not on his own religion. It appears that the curricula planners thought that the Arab child could be taught loyalty to the State of Israel by means of Jewish, Zionist and religious subject matter. In the course of time objectors to this view arose, arguing that the claim that the study of the history of Zionism and the values of Judaism will strengthen the loyalty of the Arab child to the State of Israel had not proven itself. Studies conducted in the seventies (Hoffman et al., 1978; Peres, Yuval, Davis, 1970; Smooha, in a study soon to be published) found a growing radicalization of views among young Arabs in Israel. On the other hand, there are also those who maintain that in times of war — and in fact, at all times — the Arab minority has demonstrated loyalty to the state, and the Arab youths who have been involved in terrorist activity against the state are few in number, and considering the size of the Arab population — their number is virtually nil.

Distinctive Goals

For Jewish Education: To help the youth build a whole personality as a Jew who identifies with his people's heritage and destiny, is imbued with a sense of his Jewish ancestry, imbued with an awareness of the bond between the Jewish people in its land and state and the Jewish people in the Diaspora, possessed of a sense of shared destiny and responsibility for his people. To impart the values of Jewish culture by study and practical learning of the heritage as it was formed by the Jewish people within its various communities, up until the most recent generations, in the Jewish homeland and the Diaspora. This [is to be done] along with an encounter with the best of the cultural heritage of other peoples and acquaintance with the culture of the Arab minority.

For Arab Education: To base education on the foundations of Arab culture, on the achievements of science, on the striving for peace between Israel and its neighbors, on love of the common homeland of all the citizens of the state, and on loyalty to the State of Israel. This while stressing shared interests and cultivating what is distinctive of the Arabs of Israel, and on imparting an acquaintance with Jewish culture.

For Druze Education: To base education on the values of Druze and Arab culture, on the achievements of science, in the striving for peace between Israel and its neighbors, on love of the common homeland of all the citizens of the state and loyalty to the State of Israel, on partnership in the building and defense of Israel, while stressing the special and shared interests of all its inhabitants, on fostering the special ties between Jews and Druze, on acquaintance with Jewish culture, on the cultivation of the Druze-Israeli entity, on implanting the community's heritage among the Druze youth, and on the common destiny of members of the Druze community in all the lands in which they live.

The Arab minority in Israel is not recognized as a national minority, and that being the case the educational goals for the

Arab child do not include national guidance, as do the goals for the Jewish child. Since Arab history and literature are subjects that can awaken national feelings among Arab youths, these subjects have as far as possible been emptied of national elements. Broad portions of Arab history are not taught at all, and the number of hours devoted to the study of history is limited. The Arabic language and literature curriculum does not include present-day national material, but only extracts from classical Arabic literature. The textbooks do not contain nationalist poems and the works of no Palestinian poet or writer are taught. The declared objectives of Arabic language and literature teaching for the Arab child are pragmatic ones, such as improving reading and writing skills, precision in the expression of ideas, appreciation of literature and the like. National aspects are given no heed.

Apparently, the curriculum planners thought that Arab nationalism would not promote the Arab child's loyalty to the State of Israel at a time when brothers of his, members of his people, are at war with the State of Israel — his country. However, even though Arab literature as taught has been drained of national content, and the development of national identity is not a goal of the Arab educational system in Israel, Arab pupils have indicated that these school subjects do influence their Arab identity. The Arab pupils in the study by Hoffman and others (1978) stated explicitly that these subjects (Arab literature) contribute a great deal to their national identity.

It is reasonable to suppose that the barring of expression of Arab national wishes will not eliminate or abrogate them. The Arab pupil who does not find his needs met in school will look for what he lacks — and will find it — outside the school. What is more, the avoidance of the issue of the current national awakening by the curricula and the formal educational framework consigns the national education of the Arab child in Israel to the mass media of the Arab countries. Arab high-school pupils spend a lot of time every day listening to the radio.

Sarsour (1971) and Hoffman et al. (1978) found that Arab high school pupils point to non-Israeli television programs as having a great influence on their development and education. The media of the Arab countries, of course, stress the radical components of Arab nationalism.

One of the goals of education, as we have noted, is to educate the Arab child in love of his homeland. That is one of the more problematic issues for the Arab school. It is problematic in part because the Jewish and Arab populations in Israel understand the concept "homeland" differently. The State of Israel is today perceived by the majority in Israel (the Jewish population) to be a Jewish state, and the Land of Israel is perceived to be the homeland of the Jewish people; the Jewish pupil and citizen in Israel is educated in accordance with that view. The non-Jewish citizens of Israel (the Arabs) do not have the same rights to their land as do the Jewish citizens. "For the Arabs of Israel — all rights, but to the Land of Israel — no right," wrote B.Z. Dinur, Israel's first minister of education. As a homeland, it belongs to the Jewish people. This feeling on the part of the Jewish population in Israel is not identical with the feeling of the Arab citizens. The Arabs of Israel were born in this land, they and their fathers and their fathers' fathers. They have a strong spiritual bond with and feelings for the place where they were born. They are not aliens, and the land and the soil are not alien to them. They feel that the Land of Israel is their land and home, and that they have as much, if not more of a right to it than the Jewish citizen has. In a debate between an educated Arab and a Jewish immigrant to the country, the Arab argued: "You, who arrived in the country only yesterday — the land is yours, while I and my family, who have been living here for generations — we have no right to the land?!"

The Ministry of Education and Culture has steered clear of this delicate issue. Only recently, in 1976, did the Ministry of Education and Culture gather courage and decided to educate the Arab child to love the homeland common to all the citizens of the State of Israel. This step has not yet been accompanied by a comparable step in the education of the Jewish child. As for the Jewish citizen, the Land of Israel is still the homeland only of the Jewish people, and he is not being educated to see the country as the common homeland of all the citizens of the state, regardless of religion or nationality. Because of that, educating the Arab pupil in Israel in love of the homeland is not always accepted or understood by the Jewish public. An Arab school educating its pupils in love of the homeland, for example, by taking the children on excursions, and arousing in them a good deal of patriotism, may create an image for itself of being close to circles hostile to the state. A song expressing love of the homeland sung by Arab pupils in Arabic, which declares "My land, my land, my land, my love goes out to you, my heart to you" — is dissonant to the ears of the Jews in Israel. On more than one occasion it was presented in the Hebrew mass media as an expression of Arab nationalist sentiment hostile to the state.

The Jewish-Zionist Character of the State of Israel

The State of Israel is a Jewish-Zionist state, which set as its goal the redemption of the Jewish people and the realization of Zionism. The implementation of the Zionist idea is a process not yet completed, and involves, among other things, the redemption of lands, the erection of Jewish settlements, and the maintenance of a large and clear Jewish majority in the State of Israel. There is a feeling among the Arab citizens that in the course of the realization of the Zionist idea they find themselves victimized, for example, by land expropriations and the establishment of Jewish settlements on those lands. Furthermore, the building of the state and society of Israel is being done by the Jews without the participation of the Arab citizens. The Arabs of Israel have in fact no part in the building of the Jewish society and state. They have no representation in the principal political, economic, juridical and administrative institutions in the country. What is more, even their fate and development are determined to a large extent by Jews.

Departments and bodies set up in the various government ministries to handle the affairs of Arab citizens are headed by Jews. This state of affairs cannot strengthen the Arab citizen's sense of belonging to the State of Israel. On the contrary, it tends to intensify his sense of being discriminated against. The Arabs of Israel have the feeling that the Jewish majority regards them as an alien and undesirable element. In a survey conducted among Tel-Aviv inhabitants in 1967–68, about 90 percent of the Jewish respondents stated that it would be better if there were less Arabs in the country (Peres, 1971). This being the state of affairs, some weighty educational questions arise: Can the Arab citizen in Israel be educated to identify with the Jewish state as his own? Is it possible to educate towards the integration of the Arab citizen in the State of Israel, considering that the Arab in Israel, even if he wants to, cannot be a Zionist Jew and cannot be truly incorporated in the Jewish state? Or is it better at this stage to educate primarily towards coexistence of Jews and Arabs in Israel?

Like any other country, Israel too has values and symbols with which the citizens of the country are supposed to identify: a flag, an anthem, state insignia, street names, public institutions and the like. The state also conducts social and national events and ceremonies which are supposed to heighten the citizen's identification with his country, broaden and deepen his ties with it and lift national morale.

The schools in Israel are supposed to arrange an encounter between their pupils and the symbols of the state at ceremonies, events, holidays and special days. The Arab school cannot ignore the existence of the country's symbols, and the Arab pupil in Israel must learn to know the symbols of his state. The Arab school in Israel does introduce its pupils to the symbols of the State of Israel, but the Jewish-national character of these symbols creates difficult educational problems, for these symbols do not mean the same for the Jewish and non-Jewish citizens of the country. These symbols may speak to the Jewish child; they do not speak to the Arab child. Take, for example, Israel's national anthem.

What can Arab pupils think when they sing "So long as still within our breasts, the Jewish heart beats true . . . . So long as our hopes are not yet lost — Two thousand years we cherished them . . ."? On Israel's Independence Day, too, the Arab school finds itself in a quandary, not knowing clearly what to do and how. The State of Israel's Independence Day and War of Independence do not symbolize for the Arab citizen and pupil his independence and liberation. In the eyes of the Arab parents Israel's Independence Day even has connotations the very opposite of those it has for the Jewish citizen. That being the case, the Arab school cannot insist that its pupils express feelings they do not feel and do not have, for to do so would be to educate them in hypocrisy. On the other hand, it is inconceivable that Independence Day would go by for the pupils in the Arab school, as citizens of the State of Israel, as any ordinary day; that would intensify their estrangement from the country instead of promoting their sense of belonging and loyalty to it. It may also arouse suspicions among the Jewish public and the state about the Arab school and the members of the Arab minority in general.

The Arab schools as a rule comply with the instructions of the Ministry of Education and Culture, which call upon it to celebrate that day and to stress to the pupils the achievements of the state and the achievements of the Arab sector in Israel. These programs are usually less successful in the secondary schools than in the primary schools. In the former the educational problems are most acute because of the contrasts between theory and reality which the school, with its adolescent pupil population, encounters, and which narrow its educational influence. Because of the national differences between the Arab and Jewish citizens in Israel, there are also various educational and school activities that are perceived differently by one group than by the other. It may be supposed, for example, that an excursion to liberated Jerusalem, or to the Galilee when there is much talk of the "Judaization of the Galilee," will have a different psychological and national meaning for the Jewish youth and for the Arab youth.

There are some Jewish matters that are well-received in the Arab sector, such as study of the Hebrew language. Nevertheless, the question arises, does the Arab pupil's participation in ceremonies of a Jewish national symbolic character lead to his identification with the State of Israel, with the Jewish state those symbols represent?

Segregation of Arab Education

There are two separate educational systems in Israel — for Jewish children and for Arab children. The segregation of Arab education in Israel reflects the State of Israel's liberal approach, which, in consideration for the members of the minority, allows them to provide their children with an education in the spirit of their culture and heritage. The Arab child is educated in an atmosphere similar to that in his parents' home, and thus he is spared sharp clashes between the two educational agencies — the family and the school. The Jewish school also benefits from the separation between the educational systems in the country. It is free to educate the Jewish pupil in the values of Jewish culture, it gives the Jewish pupil national and pre-military education and strengthens his identification with the Jewish people in Israel and the Diaspora.

The separation between the educational systems in Israel is favored both by the Jewish majority and by the minorities, and at no time has there been a demand from either side for the integration of Arab and Jewish education in the country. However, recently there have been many calls on the part both of

Jews and Arabs to decentralize the Arab educational system administratively and organizationally, and to incorporate the Arab schools in the various districts of the Ministry of Education and Culture according to their geographical location. Sparking this demand was mainly a desire to increase the efficiency of administrative and organizational work and to raise the level of services in the Arab schools closer to that in the Jewish schools — for in the allocation of resources the separate Arab educational system is disadvantaged as compared to the Jewish educational system.

Although the Arab educational system is a separate system, it does not have its own budget which it draws up itself; nor do the Arabs supervise its allocation and implementation. It is linked to a number of budget items in the Ministry of Education and Culture, and the various divisions of the ministry are supposed to set aside sums from their budgets for education in the Arab sector. The Department of Arab Education does not plan or draw up a budget according to its needs, which it then presents to the appropriate divisions of the Ministry of Education and Culture. The situation is just the reverse. The divisions of the Ministry of Education allocate funds to the Arab Department in an arbitrary manner, rather than on the basis of quantitative and objective criteria, and inform the Arab Department of the amount allocated (Doron, 1978). An example of bad allocation unrelated to the needs of Arab education is the allocation of resources to physical education in the Arab schools. In 1976 $2,000 were allocated for equipment and sports activities for all the Arab schools in the country. Other educational matters, especially auxiliary services such as psychological service, adult education, art education, the division for culture, and others are hardly covered at all, although the divisions responsible for these are required to give the Arab educational system service, just as they do the Jewish educational system.

It appears that the Ministry of Education and Culture allocates the minimum necessary for the continued existence of the educational framework in the Arab village, but that there is inadequate regard for the development of Arab education in the sense of improving the existing tools — equipment, buildings, teaching aids, etc.

Another prominent factor in building and equipping educational institutions in Israel is the Jewish character of the state. There are Jewish bodies and organizations in the country and elsewhere in the world that collect money and contributions for the advancement of education in Israel. These organizations, in conjunction with the government of Israel, create funds that funnel money to the Jewish educational system alone. A good reason has not yet been found for channeling a part of that money to the Arab sector, and the Arab residents of Israel do not have the possibility of raising funds from their brethren in the world or in the Arab countries for the promotion of education, in a manner similar to what the Jews do. For example, there is the Education for Israel Fund associated with the United Jewish Appeal, which acts in behalf of education in Israel. It builds comprehensive, academic, vocational and naval schools, equips them with laboratories and audio-visual aids, builds and equips sports facilities, builds and equips youth centers and libraries in development towns, gives scholarships for teacher training and for the post-primary education of needy children, and runs programs for gifted children. All that takes place, of course, only in the Jewish sector. The "stipends project" founded by the government of Israel and the Jewish Agency also operates only in the Jewish sector.

In addition, the State of Israel has built a ramified booster system to advance the weaker pupils. The pupils designated disadvantaged (*t'unei tipuah*; literally, requiring cultivation) are primarily from the Oriental Jewish communities (those of African or Asian origin). The Ministry of Education and Culture does not recognize the existence of disadvantaged pupils in the Arab sector, for the Arab pupils in Israel are not "culturally uprooted." For that reason the programs of assistance, betterment and enrichment operated in the Jewish educational system are not found in the Arab sector. The Arab citizens do not accept the position of the Ministry of Education and Culture on this and contend that the very same criteria that characterize the disadvantaged Jewish child also characterize disadvantaged Arab children. The level of education of the Arab parents is low, most Arab families live in crowded conditions, and the Arab child is not the progeny of parents who were born in America or Europe. They contend further that assistance is given the weak child because he is weak, in order to help him advance, and not because of his origin.

Furthermore, there is a dire shortage of classrooms in the Arab educational system, and the Arab schools do not benefit from the status of "maintained school,"* as in the Jewish sector. Commenting on this situation, the director-general of the Ministry of Education and Culture said: "...We cannot be at ease if the Ministry of Education and Culture, as a humane system, as a system that believes (so I hope) in the equality of the Jewish and Arab citizen in Israel, will accept what is happening today in the Arab sector, the education of which we are charged with. It has been said several times before, and if we repeat it — it should be heard and have an influence, I hope, in the very near future... It is not an impossible undertaking to set aside $2 million annually in order to provide the Arab villages with decent school conditions" (Shmueli, 1977).

It should be borne in mind that the two educational systems, the Jewish and the Arab, started off at different points. When the state was established, the Arab educational system lagged far behind the Jewish system. Today the Arab educational system operates under social conditions different from those of the Jewish system. It operates in a developing society, while the Jewish system operates in a more modern and developed society. How-

---

* A "maintained school" has its current budget covered by the Ministry, whereas other schools are maintained by the local authorities, on their budget.

ever, an unjust allocation of resources between the Arab and Jewish educational systems, not in accord with egalitarian criteria, has widened the gap between the systems instead of narrowing it. A mounting lag in a population group marked off clearly by easily recognizable features — language, religion, nationality and culture — is liable to produce social and political dangers for the future.

It should also be noted that although the educational system for Arab children is distinct, it is run by Jews. Jews head it, manage it, determine its curricula and pay its teachers and other instructional personnel. It is reasonable to suppose that because of the strong bonds of kinship between the Arabs of Israel and the Arab world, and especially with the Palestinian people (e.g., an Arab school principal in Israel is the brother of the chairman of the Palestinian National Council), the authorities do not fully trust educated Arabs, and therefore keep them out of senior posts. However, when Arabs are kept from managing the education of their children, they become suspicious of the true intentions of the Jews. Furthermore, the state, in keeping educated Arabs out of senior positions, is not preparing them for responsible positions or allowing them to rise to posts involving decision-making. That is liable to create doubts and difficulties for the educated Arab about his being an Arab citizen in a Jewish state, whereas a decision-making capacity might, on the other hand, facilitate his adaptation to life in Israel.

Because the Arab educational system is run by Jews, Arab citizens today blame the state for social and educational problems and failings in the Arab sector, although there may well be social and other reasons for them that have nothing to do with the Jewish management of the educational system. The situation is different in the Jewish sector. When problems arise or there are social or educational failings in the Jewish sector, the charges are directed against the educational system and not against the state.

The Arab Teacher in Israel

The Arabs of Israel live under the shadow of discrimination in many realms, and the educated Arabs as a group bear the frustrations of their society. Teachers make up a sizeable group within the larger body of educated Arabs; because of the difficulties in getting a position in the various government ministries or in the Jewish public sector, many Arab university graduates turn to teaching. Today, 40 percent of Arab university graduates are teachers. The Ministry of Education and Culture, too, does not always employ egalitarian criteria vis-à-vis the Arab and Jewish teachers. The Arab teacher reads in the press about various incentives, such as tax reductions and various forms of material support, offered to Jewish teachers in order to induce them to teach in development towns. By contrast, when an Arab teacher is sent by the Ministry of Education and Culture to teach the Beduin tribes in the Negev and he refuses to go, sanctions are brought to bear against him. Such a teacher may, for example, find himself boycotted by the Ministry and left without a job for two or three years. That happens, despite the fact that conditions of work and life in the Beduin tribes in the Negev are much harder than the living and working conditions in, for example, Upper Nazareth, which is considered a development town.

The practice of the Ministry of Education with regard to the Jewish teachers is understandable, given the Jewish and national goals of the State of Israel, but the feelings of deprivation and frustration that exist within certain circles of Arab teachers do not facilitate the work of educating their pupils in democratic values such as equality, tolerance and all the other goals of state education.

The teachers in the Arab schools are citizens of Israel and state employees. As such, they are expected to be loyal to the State of Israel, to identify with its goals and aspirations, and to educate the Arab pupils in good citizenship. However, since Israel has a Jewish-Zionist character, in the course of his work the

Arab educator comes up against matters and topics that are not in
his spirit, and which at times do not accord with the goals and
interests of his community in the Arab village. In such instances,
the Arab educator is torn between his loyalty to the Jewish-
Zionist state of Israel and his loyalty to his own Arab community. If he supports the state's view he is charged by his pupils
and by the community of being an "agent" of the regime and
a traitor; and if he supports the view of his Arab community
he is accused of being hostile to the state. As long as the Ministry
of Education and Culture does not demand that he take a stand
on issues over which the interests of the state clash with those
of his Arab community, the Arab teacher steers clear of these
isues and avoids discussion of them. But when the Ministry of
Education and Culture demands that the Arab teacher adopt
the official government line, and act accordingly within his class,
he does his work only because he is obliged to, and as a result
his credibility in the eyes of his pupils and his community is
tarnished. This is especially so in extreme cases in which the
Arab teacher may find himself isolated from his community, as
in the case of the Land Day strike on March 30, 1976. The
"Judaization of the Galilee" is a national goal of the State of
Israel as a Jewish country, but the expropriation of the lands of
Arab citizens in order to set up Jewish settlements on them is
not in keeping with the personal interests of Israel's Arab
citizens. On the day of the above-mentioned strike, the teachers
were told to boycott it and to work as on a regular day, and
on the morning of that day they were among the first to report
to work. In such extreme situations it also happens that some
teachers are unable to withstand the pressure of the community;
they cannot bring themselves to act in opposition to the general
atmosphere prevailing in their community and against their own
thoughts and sentiments, and diverge from the official line of the
Ministry of Education.

As a consequence of the growing number of educated Arabs,
and their greater power and rise to leadership positions in their

communities, the Arab population may be expected in the future to intensify its criticism of government policy in the Arab sector and will be less tolerant of the prejudice and discrimination it suffers — and will be less mindful of the reasons for the situation. The democratic regime in Israel allows the Arab population to express its views and to criticize the government's activities publicly. This asmosphere of criticism, of an anti-government position on the part of the Arab population, is liable to cloud the educational atmosphere in the Arab sector and in the Arab school. There are already signs of that today. On January 12, 1980, about thirty representatives of Arab local councils met in Nazareth to discuss the educational situation in the Arab sector. At the close of the meeting, they issued an announcement denouncing what they called the government's policy of national prejudice and discrimination against the Arab citizens of the country. They contended that the Ministry of the Interior takes a prejudicial stand against them and arbitrarily denies many ordinary budget requests by the Arab local authorities and charged further that the director of the Northern District was adopting a racist approach. At that same meeting it was also decided to close the Arab schools for a day, January 23, 1980, as a sign of protest. The Ministry of Education and Culture for its part demanded that teaching personnel not strike and that they teach on that day as on any other. The situation of the teachers in this case was difficult in every respect. There is no envying the Arab teacher in that position whose pupils will ask questions such as: Why aren't you striking? Why did the heads of Arab local councils call a strike? Luckily for the teachers, the strike was called off following the Ministry of Education's agreement to set aside monies for the construction of classrooms in the Arab sector.

As already noted, the Arab teachers tend to avoid discussion of political issues having to do with the relations between Israel and the Arabs. When such issues nevertheless do arise and become a topic of discussion among the pupils, especially at high school age, the pupils do sometimes address questions to their educators. The latter's evasive answers leave the pupils unsatisfied. In such cases it is doubtful that the Arab teacher can function as an educator and can impart political and social values to his pupils (Eisenstadt and Peres, 1968).

References

1. B.Z. Dinur, "Our Right to the Land of Israel" (mimeographed, in Hebrew).
2. A. Doron, Organizational Examination in the Division of Education and Culture for Arabs, Final Report, Israel Ministry of Education and Culture, 1978 (in Hebrew).
3. S.N. Eisenstadt, Y. Peres, *Some Problems of Educating a National Minority: A Study of Israeli Education for Arabs*, The Hebrew University of Jerusalem, Jerusalem, 1968.
4. Y. Hoffman, R. Hertz-Lazarovitch, N. Ruhana, B. Beit-Halahmi, "The Influence of School Subjects on the Formation of the Identity of Jewish and Arab Pupils in Israel," *'Iyunim B'hinuch 19* (1978), 153–169, School of Education, University of Haifa (in Hebrew).
5. Y. Peres, "Ethnic Relations in Israel," *American Journal of Sociology 76(6)* (1971), 1021–1047.
6. Y. Peres and N. Yuval-Davis, "Attitudes of Arab Pupils Towards Jews as Individuals and Towards Israel as a State," *Megamot 17* (1970), 258–260 (in Hebrew).
7. Y. Peres, A. Ehrlich and N. Yuval-Davis, "National Education of Arab Youth in Israel: A Comparison of Curricula," *Megamot 16* (1968), 26–37 (in Hebrew).
8. S. Sarsour, "Leisure and its Uses, A Study of Patterns of Leisure Use by Arab High School Pupils in the Triangle," School of Education, Bar-Ilan University, 1971 (in Hebrew).
9. E. Shmueli, "The Ministry's Tasks for the 1977–78 School Year," in: *Hamefaqeah Umesimot Hamisrad*, The Pedagogical Secretariat, Israel Ministry of Education and Culture, 1977, pp. 7–18 (in Hebrew).

Chapter V

THE IDENTITY PROBLEM
OF THE
ARAB MINORITY

THE POLITICIZATION OF ISRAEL'S ARABS

ELI REKHESS

The beginning of the 1980s has seen an acceleration of the process of political radicalization among the Arab population of Israel. This process has been fueled by two sources: socioeconomic change, and political developments in the Middle East since 1967.

There have been dramatic changes in the structure of social and economic life among the Arabs in Israel since the establishment of the State in 1948, due partly to the government's development policy. Several features of this change are noteworthy:

1. Demographic growth. The high rate of natural increase of the population (close to 4 per cent annually, compared to about 1.8 per cent among the Jews) generates a feeling of strength and self-confidence.

2. Rise in standard of living. The development of infrastructure services in the Arab village, the "green revolution" in Arab agriculture, which has become mechanized and modern, the absorption of Arab manpower in the services and industry — all led to a substantial rise in income levels and standard of living.

3. Social restratification. The development of the educational system, at all levels, contributed to the emergence of a new social

stratum — the young and educated. The thousands of Arab high-school graduates, university students and university graduates are gradually superseding the representatives of the old, traditional generation, and replacing them as the leaders of Arab society. The family and the clan are yielding their power to larger, more national frameworks. The educated class bases its strength more on personal achievement than on ascriptive criteria (family origin and inherited economic wealth).

4. Rise in level of expectations. The Arab sector's almost exclusive model for assessing its situation is the level of development of the Jewish population. Such comparison reveals sizeable gaps between the two sectors. These gaps are most marked in areas such as industrialization, housing, lands, education and job opportunities for professionals. Perceived inequities in these areas have precipitated a deep crisis of trust in relations with the authorities, accompanied by feelings of frustration, bitterness, alienation and estrangement. Feelings of prejudice and discrimination on the civic plane are channeled by political bodies onto the national plane.

Developments in this sphere have had dramatic implications for the national identity of the Arabs of Israel. The conditions that prevailed until the Six-Day War allowed for the maintenance of a delicate balance between belonging to the Arab nation and being citizens of Israel. The physical severance from the Arab world, the political and diplomatic deadlock in the region and the existence of the Military Government all encouraged broad sections of the Arab population to reconcile themselves to the situation, with the hope that change would come from the outside.

The Six-Day War reshuffled the cards. The renewed encounter with the Arabs of Judea, Samaria and Gaza and the restoration of ties with the Arab world altered the status quo. The sense of Palestinian identity and the feeling of belonging to the Arab world grew stronger. The broad nationalist activity in the territories, together with criticism of the extent of the Israeli Arabs' loyalty to the Palestinian Arab nationality exacerbated the crisis of national identity, which was now subjected to new pressures. At the same time, Israel's military superiority and deterrent strength prevented the Arab countries from effecting any change, forestalling a total collapse of the moderate outlook that advocated preservation of the status quo.

The Yom Kippur War caused a fundamental alteration in this view of things. The rehabilitation of Arab honor did not leave the Arabs of Israel unaffected. With the shattering of the image of a "mighty Israel," the image of the Arab world grew stronger. Doubts spread among the Arab public about Israel's invincibility, contributing to their increased self-confidence. The rise of the PLO after 1973 marked another important step in the reinforcement of the Israeli Arabs' sense of Palestinianness. A two-way process was begun: growing regard by the Arabs of Israel for the PLO as a representative framework, with the PLO, for its part, paying more and more attention to the Arabs of Israel with the objective of incorporating them in the general Palestinian national struggle. This was clearly manifest in the fight against land expropriations in the Galilee (Land Day) and in the municipal elections in Nazareth in 1975. In the course of the process and the events that accompanied it the solidarity between the Arabs of Israel and the Arabs of the territories increased.

As a result of the above, a substantial change has occurred in the political stance of the Arabs of Israel. The moderate camp has been forced to radicalize its position and join those who stress the Palestinian national identity. The activity of the Zionist parties (Labor, Mapam, National Religious) in the Arab sector is almost inconsequential, and the incentives these parties had provided for the moderate camp are now virtually meaningless. The moderate camp has been seriously weakened by the rise of radical groups such as the Villagers' Movement, and the Progressive National Movement. The devotees of these groups — especially the young and educated among them — demand the right of self-determination for the Israeli Arabs. They view the PLO — in all its factions, including the rejectionist front — as the sole

legitimate representative of the Palestinians; call for the establishment of a vigorous national authority in the territories as an
interim solution without peace, recognition of Israel or negotia-
tions, and support the establishment of a democratic, secular
state. Mention should also be made of the movement of young
Moslems representing a radical stream influenced by the Islamic
awakening in the Arab and Moslem world. This group's strength
is on the rise.

The major political camp among the Arabs of Israel is Rakah
[the New Communist List]. The Communists reject the demand
that the Arabs of Israel be granted the right to self-determination,
and view themselves as part of the state. At the same time, they
also support the major faction in the PLO, Fatah, and regard the
organization as the sole representative of the Palestinian people.
They advocate the establishment of an independent state in the
territories, alongside Israel. Rakah, which organizationally is well
entrenched among the Arab public, is today on the offensive
against the attacks of the radical Arab groups who maintain that
Rakah is too moderate and that it must adopt a more extreme
stand.

The political radicalization of the Arabs of Israel feeds on the
developments in the two realms we have noted, and the consequences of the social, economic and political changes in their
society are closely interwoven.

One of the important consequences of this process is the
transition to a behavioral pattern of political activism by the
Arabs of Israel. This activism is manifest in a decision to do
battle against the government, while striving for a confrontation
on civil-rights matters related, for example, to education or land
expropriation. This change was given forceful expression in
March 1976, by the events of Land Day, which was organized as
a protest against land expropriations in the Galilee.

Israel's Arabs conduct their struggle within the bounds of the
law, exploiting the legitimate political activity accorded by Israeli democracy (municipal elections, Knesset elections). Nation-

wide action bodies, separate from established political frameworks, are set up to advance the common struggle of interest groups dispersed over various geographical areas. A national committee of Arab students has been formed, as has a national committee of heads of local councils and another for the defense of lands. Rakah is a moving force behind this form of organization, operating in accord with the classic Communist method of setting up "fronts" which bring representatives of various sectors together under one roof. Gradually, the distinction between the struggles for civil rights and national rights has been obscured, the framework itself becoming part of the national struggle of the Palestinians under Israeli rule (in the territories), and more broadly, of the overall struggle of the PLO. Against the background of these developments, local government in the Arab sector became a focus of political power, an instrument for promoting local interests and a tool used by politicians and political groups for acquiring a national power and influence base. This is reflected in the high voting rates in Arab municipal elections, with as much as 80 and 90 per cent of the eligible voters casting their ballots. The proportion of young educated Arabs on local councils has gradually and steadily increased and the older generation is being pushed out of power positions. Although many of the electoral lists still have a family or clan character, the share of the independent or party lists has risen. The separation between the elections for head of council and for council members has helped to stabilize the municipal system although it has not altogether neutralized features from the past, namely the seesawing of power between rival groups, the frequent ousters and recriminations, which symbolize the instability that has its roots in the traditional social structure.

The Zionist parties operating in the Arab sector have little influence. Rakah's presence, on the other hand, is widely felt. It engages in intensive activity by way of an excellent organizational network that reaches into most of the Arab villages. Recently, "fronts" have begun to be set up jointly with political bodies not affiliated with the Communist Party. A coalition of this sort was formed towards the end of 1975 in Nazareth, where Rakah and its partners won the mayoralty elections. In the 1978 municipal elections this trend was taken further. Using fronts, Rakah won 19 of 51 council-head positions. Before that, only 10 councils were headed by Rakah men. Prior to 1978 the fronts had 51 representatives on 21 councils; as a result of the elections that year its representation rose to 109 councilmen on 36 councils.

Rakah channels its attempts to broaden its influence through two other bodies mentioned above: the National Committee of Heads of Arab Local Councils and the Committee for the Defense of Arab Lands.

The National Committee of Heads of Local Councils was formed in 1974 in order to act on the local plane, primarily in bringing grants of the Ministry of Interior to Arab local councils in line with those issued to Jewish councils. The events of 1976 — the expropriation of lands in the Galilee and the strike that was called for March 30, 1976 — gave the committee a big boost and helped to establish its representative status, so successfully that it is now sometimes called the "parliament of the Israeli Arabs." Since the mid-seventies, the activity of the Committee has branched off into two directions:

a. A broadening of its field of operation to include Israeli Arab national issues and general Palestinian matters, while demonstrating its involvement in what is going on in Judea, Samaria and the Gaza Strip.

b. An extension of its aegis to a wide set of social and economic problems of Israeli Arabs on the village level related to building, planning, taxation, education, water, sewage, sanitation, medicine, housing, industrialization and the like.

The heads of the Committee claim that they are not a political body, and certainly not a party. The government ministries, however, do not recognize the Committee, and its activists are therefore trying to gain a standing within the Local Government Center, the establishment framework to which they wish to belong.

Another body in which Rakah plays a central role is the National Committee for the Defense of Arab Lands, which was founded in the latter part of 1975 against a background of rumors about government intentions to expropriate Arab lands in the Galilee. The Committee interpreted the government's decision to seize about 20,000 dunams of land in the Galilee for development purposes — only 6,000 of these dunams were Arab-owned — as dispossession of the Arabs and usurpation of their homeland. It wasn't long before the boundaries between a protest action by citizens against their government and a distinctly national struggle became blurred. With all the declarations being made then about the Judaization of the Galilee — as the program was originally called — it was easy for the Rakah activists to unite representatives of various sectors within the Arab population under one roof. It was this body that led the fight against the expropriations, culminating in the general strike organized for Land Day.

Since 1976, the activity of the committee has branched out into three directions:

a. Broadening and institutionalizing the organizational base in the Arab villages.

b. Widening the field of activity to all matters related to "land." Thus, the committee took under its aegis the struggle against the demolition of buildings and structures erected without legal permits and organized a wide range of protest actions against activities of this sort by the government. The Committee has likewise intervened in the Negev Beduins' struggle against their eviction from areas where new airfields are to be built (replacing those relinquished in the Sinai), and has engaged in protest activities against the establishment of small Jewish hilltop settlements in the Galilee and against the policy of the "Green Patrol."

c. Adoption of a line of non-violent political action. In the years since the first Land Day, there has been no recurrence of the bloody clashes between Arab citizens and the security forces that took place on March 30, 1976. Since then the Committee has chosen to mark Land Day by quiet protest, especially by holding memorial assemblies for the six who were killed in 1976. The decision for non-violent protest was apparently guided by the fear that a general strike and demonstrations would provoke a counter-response from extremist Jewish circles and would create hostile Jewish public opinion that would encourage the authorities to take measures against the Committee; another reason for the choice of non-violence was apparently the desire to demonstrate leadership ability and control.

Since 1979 the heads of the Committee have been finding it difficult to maintain this course under pressure from groups such as the Villagers' Movement, which call for the adoption of a more militant line. The Committee's position is difficult in that, on the one hand, it wishes to stay within the bounds of the law in order not to be driven out of existence, while on the other hand, its status and influence have begun to be eroded by the radicals. In consequence, the Committee has been forced to radicalize its positions by broadening its range of reference to national political issues and, for example, expressing solidarity with the fate of the inhabitants of the occupied territories and with the struggle of the Palestinian Arab people. Thus, in a broadsheet issued on March 30, 1979, the Committee asserted that it was necessary to declare to the world that peace is impossible without recognition of the rights of the Palestinian people to establish an independent state alongside Israel, together with Israel's immediate withdrawal to its pre-1967 boundaries.

THE PROBLEM OF IDENTITY IN THE
LITERATURE OF THE ISRAELI ARABS

GEORGE KANAZI

There are many studies that deal with the identity of the Arabs of Israel, especially from the points of view of political scientists, psychologists, sociologists and educators. Researchers in these and other fields have been interested in this subject because of its implications for the image of the Israeli Arab, and for relations between Jews and Arabs in the State of Israel. Smooha and Cibulski's annotated bibliography covers about 430 studies from different disciplines, a good many of them directly concerned with the problem of the national identity of the Arabs of Israel.[1]

These studies rely in the main on official documents and papers or on questionnaires especially composed in order to bare the position of the person questioned on some specific point. What follows here is based not on empirical studies conducted in the field but on Arabic literature in Israel, which clearly reflects the problems, thoughts, hopes and national identity of the Arabs of Israel.

It is important to note that Arabic literature in Israel has not

1 Sammy Smooha and Ora Cibulski, *Social Research on Arabs in Israel, 1948–1977, Trends and Annotated Bibliography*, Turtledove Publishing, Ramat Gan, 1978.

yet been the subject of comprehensive and thorough research, apparently because of its limited artistic merit (save for several exceptional works). Those who did deal with this literature — such as Avraham Yanun in the sixties[2] and Shimon Ballas in his book on "Arabic Literature in the Shadow of War,"[3] that was published in 1978 — did so because of the social and political topics it takes up. Like them, I too will refrain from dealing with the artistic aspects or merits of this literature, and the excerpts I cite are brought not as examples of outstanding creation but to substantiate the points being made. It should be noted here that one of the major characteristics of this literature is that it consists mostly of poetry, though in recent years collections of short stories, novels and plays have also appeared.

The soul of the Arab living in Israel is split between his people and the state in which he lives. That fact is not a source of much gratification. The Israeli-Arab conflict, which began before 1948, still continues, and as a consequence of it the Arab in Israel feels he is in a very special situation; he must work out a compromise for maintaining these clashing loyalties — to his Arab people and to his Jewish state. That is what gives rise to the problem of identity, or more accurately, of identification with one side or the other. For virtually no one will deny that the Arabs of Israel regard themselves as part of the great Arab nation in the midst of which the State of Israel was established. Before 1948 they were the majority, but after the state was established they became a national minority living in a country which takes the realization of Zionism to be its raison d'être.

Arabic literature in Israel reveals feelings of pride and honor about the Arab identity. In many poems the poets take pride

---

2 Avraham Yanun, "Some Focal Topics in the Literature of the Arabs of Israel," *Hamizrah Hahadash* 15 (1965), 57–84 (in Hebrew); "Social Topics in the Literature of the Arabs of Israel," *Hamizrah Hahadash* 16 (1966), 349–380.

3 Shimon Ballas, *Hasifrut Ha'aravit Batzel Hamilhama*, Am Oved, Tel-Aviv, 1978.

in their Arabness and glory in the scientific and cultural achievements of the Arabs in the past, on the one hand comparing this
glorious past with the wretched past of the Western world, and
on the other, with the wretched present of the Arab world. Here
the poet sings out, takes pride and criticizes not as an outsider
but as in every way an Arab entitled both to swell with pride
and to criticize.

In a poem from 1968 called "The Revolt of the Singer with
Rabāba Accompaniment" (the *rabāba* is a one- or two-stringed
Oriental musical instrument), Samiḥ al-Qāsim extols the past of
the Arabs, who began their career as a people with the appearance of Muhammed 1400 years ago. For a thousand years they
built large cities, centers of culture and science, universities,
libraries, gardens, etc., while Europe was culturally at a very low
ebb. But these achievements were possible only so long as the
power of improvisation did not characterize the East, as it does
today. That greatness came to an end, and all that remains are
stories one has tired of hearing over and over again. Therefore,
the poet concludes his poem saying:

> If our children would understand what is broadcast on the
> many radio stations
> And the claptrap about plans grand and small, they would
> weep!
> Our children would weep if they understood the "import-
> ant talks"
> In councils of ministers... in preparation for summit
> conferences!
> O my nation!
> Utter what is on your lips! Are you not a nation?
> Come back, for the tongue is weary and gone are the
> newspaper readers;
> Come back! The old singer wants to change the song!
> O my nation! Offer this *rabāba*
> Something other than excellence in speech-making:

Offer a new tune
And give to posterity new deeds of glory.[4]

Following the same line of thought, in a biting poem, Samiḥ al-
Qāsim derides the "army of rescue" that was defeated in 1948,
and while doing so points critical barbs against tradition, modes
of education, and the holding on to useless beliefs. Rebelling
against tradition, he cries out:

O defeated father, O demeaned mother
The tribal heritage you bequeathed me
I dispatch to Hell.[5]

But despite the criticism that he himself levels, and that can be
called "domestic criticism," he rails against all "foreign criticism" that seeks to scoff at or deride the Arabs. For example,
when the enemy says: "They are barbarians, they are Arabs,"
Mahmoud Darwish responds:

We are Arabs
And not ashamed of it!
We know how to grasp the scythe handle
And how he who is unarmed defends himself!
We know how to build a modern factory
... a house
Hospital
School
Bomb
Rocket!
And we write
Beautiful music and songs
Gleaming and suffused with thought and feeling.[6]

4   Samiḥ al-Qāsim, *Dukhān al-Barākin*, Nazareth, 1968, pp. 73–74.
5   *Ibid.*, p. 93.
6   Mahmoud Darwish, *'Ashiq Min Falastin*, Nazareth, 1968, pp. 73–74.

The feeling of identification with the greater Arab people is even more marked in works that refer to various events in the Arab world, such as the Sinai War in 1956, the Algerian revolt in 1954–1962, the events in Lebanon in 1958, the coup d'état in Iraq in 1958 that toppled the crown there, the revolt in Oman in the seventies, and others. The Arab identity of the Arab writer living in Israel is thereby stressed.

However, that apparently was too broad an identity, which did not provide a sufficiently crystalized or clearly enough defined feeling. Thus, Ḥannā Abū Ḥannā asks the question: Who are we? and answers it by saying:

> We are part of our wandering people!
> We are but a planting of its scattered field
> We are one of its wounds not yet bandaged.[7]

The term "our wandering people" does not refer to the Arabs in general, but to the people who made up the majority of the population of Palestine until 1948, most of whom became refugees after the establishment of the State of Israel — the Palestinian people. Arabic literature in Israel of the fifties and sixties speaks often about the refugees, the injustice done them, their great suffering, the homeland that was split in two, as also happened to the people, and the hope that a day would come when justice would triumph over injustice and the people would return to its homeland.

Interestingly, the literature that describes the sundering of the people, the refugees and their suffering, and the hope for the ultimate victory of justice, mentions the homeland and the Palestinian identity, but does not make a point of it. There is a lot of talk of "the people" and "the nation" but not yet as a defined and crystalized identity. The first period in the history of Arabic literature in Israel, from 1948 to 1965, can thus be called a period of groping.

---

7   Ḥannā Abū-Ḥannā, *Nidā' al-Jirāḥ*, Amman, 1969, p. 90.

After 1948 there was a brief period of almost total silence, which came to an end in the early fifties. The writers came to discern a new political reality: Israel as an established fact and as a state that regarded its goal to be the implementation and realization of Zionism. In an attempt to adjust to that new reality, some writers joined the Communist Party. They used the party press to publish their literary works, which sharply criticized what to them seemed the ruthlessness of the new regime, the oppressive rule and the tremendous pressure being put on the Arabs who remained in the country. Other writers observed that the Jewish majority in Israel was not a single homogeneous group, but was composed of diverse groups engaged in a debate about the structure, ideological foundation and image of the State of Israel. These writers thought it possible to find a basis for life together by cooperating with Jewish leftist forces, especially with Mapam. That is the background for understanding the activity of the poets Rashid Hussein, Omar Zu'bi, Fawzi al-Asmar and others who, believing in the success of their idea, devoted much time and energy to a joint Jewish-Arab struggle and wrote about this possibility in Mapam's Arabic newspaper and in its periodicals, *al-Mirṣād* and *al-Fajr*. There were other poets who operated in conjunction with the Histadrut clubs in the Arab sector; they too believed in the possibility of peaceful coexistence and were much encouraged in this by those in charge of these clubs. As can be seen, despite the different approaches of various groups of writers to the issue of majority-minority relations in the country, they all hoped that equality, cooperation and mutual respect would prevail in the relations between the various parts of the population, and between Jews and Arabs throughout the East.

In a competition for the "Brotherhood Cup" conducted by the journal *al-Mujtama'* in 1956, many poets extolled what the two peoples held in common, called for the animosity of the past to be forgotten and for a new era of good neighborly relations to be begun, as befit the members of one family. Addressing a

Jewish poet, Rāshid Hussein, the winner of the competition, said:

> Should the bitter, senseless, bloody memories
> Arise in your mind.
> Turn away from them, don't recall them
> Pave a lighted path for the morrow that is coming.[8]

Many other poets expressed similar hopes on various occasions. But at the same time those hopes were being fostered, other factors were also at work, pulling in a different direction. The national feeling of the Israeli Arabs was directly influenced by the Sinai campaign in 1956, and the slaughter of fifty innocent people in Kafr Kassem just prior to the campaign; the emergence of Nasser as the leader of Arab nationalism and the split between him and 'Abd al-Karim Qāsim, the leader of the Iraqi coup d'état in 1958; the events in Lebanon in 1958; Mapam's entry into the Mapai-led coalition, which disappointed many of the Arabs who had worked for cooperation with Jewish leftist forces.

Still, it must be noted that the major factor influencing Arabic literature in Israel, its content and the pointedness of its expression, was daily life in Israel. In an article written in 1965, Avraham Yanun reviewed the content of a story by Tawfiq Mu'amar (published in Nazareth in 1959) that deals with the situation of the Arabs in Israel in the late fifties. The story pointed out the sectors in which discrimination against the Arabs was clearly evident (development plans, tax policy, employment, etc.), as it did point out the Arabs' outcry against the Military Government, land expropriations, Judaization of the Galilee, and the uprooting of people from their land. Summing up this chapter, Yanun says that the government of Israel appears in this story as uninterested in the welfare of the Arabs in any area. On the con-

---

8 Rāshid Hussein, *al-Mujtama'* 3 (12), December, 1956, p. 19; see also pp. 20–21.

trary, it is a government that is weaving plots to dispossess them and to uproot them from their land, all by means of the Military Government."[9]

Because of this policy the authors developed the motif of "pressure and resistance." Poets wrote a good deal about it and expressed themselves in an extremely acid manner when dealing with the subjects that weighed upon them. Thus, for example, the Kafr Kassem massacre was described as an intentional act designed to frighten the Arabs into fleeing from their homeland; the response, accordingly, was, "Don't leave the homeland." In his poem "Death for Nothing," Mahmoud Darwish blesses those killed in Kafr Kassem for their blood-drenched glory, and ends the poem saying "we shall remain"; the tombstones on the graves of the victims are "the hand that holds us."[10] The same poet returns to the idea of resistance to pressure in another poem called "The Reply," in which he asserts that the resistance to oppression is like a holy rite, for which he is ready to die. He says: "If I burn on the cross of my rite, I become a martyr in fighter's form." Tawfiq Zayyād similarly stresses the clinging to the homeland despite all pressures. We are ready for everything, he says, to do all kinds of dirty work, to eat dust even, to sacrifice our blood, but we shall not leave.[12] Fawzi 'Abdallah is even thankful for this pressure, since, because of it "we have learned to stand firm."[13]

One of the problems of the Arabs of Israel many writers have dealt with and which is of special interest is the problem of land. The land is perceived as a fundamental element in a person's identity. This conception is expressed by many writers. In his thorough and interesting study of "Arabic Literature In the Shadow of War," Shimon Ballas analyzes a short story by

9   Avraham Yanun, *Hamizrah Hahadash* 15, 61.
10 Mahmoud Darwish, *Akhir al-layl*, Acre, 1967, pp. 77–80.
11 *Ibid.*, pp. 116–117.
12 Tawfiq Zayyād, *Ashud 'Alā Ayādikum*, Haifa, 1969, pp. 127–128.
13 Fawzi Abdallah, *Maw'id ma' al-Matar*, Nazareth, 1966, p. 13.

Tawfik Zayyād about the flight from the homeland in 1948. In this story the narrator draws a comparison between the people who fled from the homeland for fear of their lives and the dog they took with them to the Nablus area, who one day managed to slip away from his owners and return to the village whence he had come. Ballas asserts that the author gave "expression to the nationalist conception that has taken root among the Arab population in Israel, and which is manifest mainly in poetry, a conception that rests on the principle of clinging to the land."[14] This conception had in fact crystalized before the establishment of the state, and can be seen in the Palestinian literature of the Mandatory period. With the renewal of the literary life of the Palestinians who remained in Israel, it again came to the fore and produced a literature "and mainly poetry, militant in nature and suffused with nationalist pathos," as Ballas states.[15]

The land in question is the individual's private property, where he lives and which he works for his and his family's subsistence. But it is also the homeland in which the nation as a whole lives and maintains its natural way of life. For Mahmoud Darwish the homeland is the soil from which he has grown and over which his heart hovers like a bee.[16] This homeland, which has been divided into two, as has the nation, suffers from oppression, from a tear that must be mended. This tear affects the individual's identity, and for that reason many writers speak of mending it. Fawzi al-Asmar defines the right of the Palestinians to mend that tear in the following way:

> My right it is that we see the sun
> That we destroy the black tent of
> Exile
> And eat olives and water the vineyard
> With our song;

14 Shimon Ballas, *Hasifrut Ha'aravit . . .*, p. 39.
15 *Ibid.*, p. 52.
16 Mahmoud Darwish, *Akhir al-Layl*, pp. 110–112.

Above the hills of Jaffa and Haifa
We will sing the song of love,
Plant love in our green earth
That is my right
And I will rest in the shade of nothing but that right.[17]

That this right is not realized affects the national feeling of the writer. This is expressed in two ways. One is through the feeling of estrangement, and the personal sense that he is an alien in his own homeland, as expressed by Fawzi al-Asmar, Fawzi 'Abdallah and Na'īm 'Arāydi.[18] The second is by very sharp attacks against the Government of Israel's domestic and foreign policies and against the Arab countries. Since 1965, when A. Yanun wrote his survey of the topics engaging Arabic literature in Israel, the image of the Israeli government held by Arab authors has remained essentially unchanged. This government, which for Arab authors symbolizes a regime of ruthless repression, continues to disregard the Arab citizens of the country. It should be noted, however, that the Israeli Arab poet distinguishes between the rulers of Israel and the Jewish people. The criticism directed against the rulers is not the product of nation-hatred; it is an expression of bitterness towards an oppressive regime which removed a people from its land, and then took over that land. Tawfiq Zayyād stretches out his hand to the people, to the workers who are his fellow wayfarers, and declares:

I do not hate even one Jew
For nation hatred is not in my blood;
Even if his rulers ravish my people and homeland
I place my heart and mouth
In the service of both peoples ... until victory.[19]

17 Fawzi Al-Asmar, *Dāmouniyāt*, Nazareth, 1971, pp. 25–26.
18 Fawzi Al-Asmar, *Ard al-Mi'ād*, Acre, 1969, p. 22; Fawzi Abdallah, *Maw'id ma' al-Maṭar*, p. 55; Na'im 'Araydi, *Athdā Wa-Qubūr*, Nazareth, n.d., pp. 81–82, 84.
19 Tawfiq Zayyād, *Sujanā' al-Huriyah*, Nazareth, 1973, pp. 81–82.

Many events since 1965 have deepened and sharpened national sentiment among the Arabs of Israel and their identification with the Palestinians and with the Arabs in general. The establishment of the Palestinian Liberation Organization (1964) and the June 1967 war came at the beginning of the second period, in which the works of Arab writers here are characterized by their bitter tone.

The social problems Yanun surveyed in this period became secondary concerns. Although the June 1967 war was indeed disastrous for the Arab armies, the Arab writers thought it very important that following Israel's victory the masks that had previously covered its face had now been removed. Israel unmasked appeared in its true form as the faithful servant of imperialism, with its interest in oil from the East. The Arabs build the High Dam and plan to build schools, factories, etc., and Israel attacks from the side, for it fears these development plans. The Arabs, who had pleaded their case to the Security Council for twenty years to no avail, already learned the lesson; therefore, Samih al-Qāsim, addressing the Security Council in a poem already quoted above, says:

> O same old Security Council
> My voice reaches you like a red flower
> From the scene of the crime
> See you ... See you
> Old Security Council
> See you in Old Jerusalem.[20]

He believes that on June 5 "we were born anew."[21] By this new birth he meant the joining with the forces of the left that operate in broad daylight, for they believe in man wherever he is.[22]

---

20 Samih al-Qāsim, *wa-Yakūn an ya'tī Tā'r al-Ra'd*, Acre, 1969, pp. 5–12.
21 *Ibid.*, p. 140.
22 *Ibid.*, p. 126.

Tawfiq Zayyād too failed to view the June defeat as the end of everything. For him it was one step backwards in preparation for ten steps forward.[23] After the war there arose the question of the occupied territories. The Arab governments demanded total withdrawal from all the territories, and Arabic literature in Israel reflected the same position: the Israeli army is a conquering force which must be removed from the conquered homeland.[24] The day will yet come when the song of freedom will be sung in East Jerusalem, Gaza and the Golan Heights — when the occupation will be a matter of the past.[25] In Zayyād's view, the annexation of land by force is no guarantee of security, and he asks:

> What mother bequeathed you
> Half the Canal?
> What mother bequeathed you Jordan's bank
> Sinai and those mountains?
> Who robs a right by warring
> How will he defend that right
> When the scales tip?[26]

Israel must leave the territories not only for those reasons, but also because the United Nations adopted a resolution calling for Israel's withdrawal. Those nations, the sage judges, ruled what they ruled, but the vagrant child, Israel, goes on drumming, not caring a whit, even when the children's judge hangs himself — as Jamāl Qa'wār writes.[27]

After analyzing several Palestinian literary texts produced in Israel and outside it, Ballas reached the conclusion that the crystalization of the national consciousness among the Palestinians took place in various lands. For the Arabs of Israel this

---

23 Tawfiq Zayyād, *Sujanā' al-Ḥuriyah*, p. 42.
24 *Ibid.*, p. 15.
25 *Ibid.*, pp. 23–26.
26 *Ibid.*, p. 37.
27 Jamāl Qa'wār, *Ghubār al-Safar*, Nazareth, 1973, p. 44.

consciousness was formed from "the daily contact with Israeli reality, and was expressed, under the guidance of leftist forces, as a system of identification with the scattered members of the people and with the Arab nation as a whole, as part of an effort to preserve the unique character of a national minority clinging to its land and to the values of its culture... Among the refugees this consciousness was formed from a long experience of disappointment and degradation in the host countries."[28]

The hostile attitude of some Arab leaders towards the Palestinians has also been given serious treatment in the local literature. The events of "black September" in Amman in 1970 led to very sharp responses in the local literature. In the eyes of Jamāl Qa'wār, King Hussein is a tyrant who kills babies, fearing they may grow up to fight against him. The thousands killed that September were a great but not excessive sacrifice for the ultimate objective. Alluding to the many who fell in the Algerian revolt against the French, Qa'wār asks:

> What is the high price now, my wounded homeland?
> Twenty thousand?
> Others have sacrificed a million!
> And the voice of vengeance echoes: Water me
> Until over the seven hills
> Nero's body be torn.[29]

The events in the Tel Za'tar refugee camp in Lebanon are the subject of a story by Muhammed Ali Taha. The story, an allegory on the various Arab leaders and the way they treat the Palestinian problem, tells of a young boy who constantly recalls and longs for his village. This youth is wounded in the Phalangist attacks on the camp, and as his wounds are being dressed he promises that if the people of the camp will stand fast against the attacks he will get back to the homeland.[30]

28 Shimon Ballas, *Hasifrut Ha'aravit . . .*, p. 52.
29 Jamāl Qa'wār, *Al-Riḥ W'al-Shirā'*, Jerusalem, 1973, p. 20.
30 Muhammed 'Alī Ṭāha, *'Āid al-Mi'āri*, Acre, 1978, pp. 9–16.

On the basis of these two works, it appears that in case
of a conflict between the Palestinians and an Arab host country,
the Israeli-Arab writer will identify with the Palestinians. Need-
less to say, that would also be his position in a conflict with
Israel. A different tone emerges from a poem by Samiḥ al-Qāsim
in which he describes a shepherd roaming with his flock in some
beautiful part of the homeland. One day that shepherd, with a
flute in his hand, was killed and the Israeli press reported: "The
police found a dead terrorist."[31] The poet obviously does not
believe the official Israeli announcements about terrorists killed
on the border. Those dead are simple innocent people who are
killed wantonly.

In summary, the problem of identity in Arabic literature in
Israel was treated in two ways. In the first period, which ended
in 1965, the emphasis was on Arabism, and the identification
therefore was with the Arab world as a whole, but also with the
Palestinian people as a secondary identification. In the second
period the Palestinian identity takes the prime place, after events
led to its crystalization. That identity is actualized only by clinging to the land, for without land there is no existence. It is not
surprising, then, that land became the central topic in the local
literature, especially after Land Day on March 30, 1976. Because
the land is so crucial to identity, Suleiman Dagash called his collection of poems *My Identity is the Land*, and in the opening poem
likened the land to a mother nursing her children, who in turn
remain faithful to her.[32] Jamāl Qa'wār, too, holds that the land
is a mother, not to be sold, even for the highest price, for it is a
symbol of the nation's unity.[33]

Land Day in 1976 had many echoes in the local literature and
became a symbol of fidelity to the land. Thus, the poet Ali
al-Siḥ chose to call his collection of poems *Best Wishes Every*

---

31 Samiḥ al-Qāsim, *Al-Mawt al-Kabīr*, Haifa, 1973, p. 89.
32 Suleiman Dagash, *Hawiyati al-Arḍ*, Acre, 1979, p. 5.
33 Jamāl Qa'wār, *Aqmār Fi Droub al-Layl*, Acre, 1979, p. 48.

March. In this collection, which does not contain much fine poetry, the rage sparked by the land expropriations is almost palpable. To illustrate, I quote several lines:

> Write to the minister of crime
> That the bombs of Golani*
>
> And the rifles of the Border Guard
> Have carried out a death sentence,
> Burned bodies;
> Write! Write! Write!
> That our villages tore the flags
> And the caps of Golani
> And the caps of the Border Guard
> Have been trampled underfoot in my homeland.[34]

This rage stems from the Arab's failure to accept that he will in fact benefit from the land seizures. He believes that these seizures are just another attempt to strike at him and his existence. That is the principal motif in the play, *Al Natour*, by Salim Makhūlī.[35] In this play, land is expropriated in order make way for a new Jewish settlement. Interestingly, despite the tensions ensuing from the expropriation the authors appear optimistic about the future. The oppression will come to an end. This optimistic tone is the product of a deep rooted faith and the belief that a just and persistent struggle must bear fruit. But it is also the product of a Marxist belief that everything is in constant motion and therefore must change for the better. Thus, "the land does not complete one round without a new victory,"[36] as Samih al-Qāsim put it.

Many of the more prominent writers in the local literature are what Ballas calls "enlisted" writers; that is, Communist writers working in the framework of a party that has a clear ideology

---

* A crack Israeli infantry unit.

34 Ali al-Siḥ, *Kul Ādhār wa-Antum bi-Khayr*, Acre, 1977, pp. 59–60.

35 Salīm Makhūlī, *Al-Nāṭour*, Haifa, 1979.

36 Samiḥ al-Qāsim, *Iram*, Haifa, 1965, p. 50.

which it tries to "sell." Emil Habibi, who wrote "The Six-Day Sextet," Tawfiq Zayyād, Samiḥ al-Qāsim, Salem Jubrān and others are in this category. Identity for them exists on two different planes: the local plane, where it is expressed as identification with their people, who are disadvantaged and fighting for freedom; and the universal plane, where it is expressed as identification with the struggle of all peoples who are in conflict with foreign forces — i.e., imperialism. The Israeli-Arab conflict and the struggle of the Palestinian people are just one link in the struggle of all oppressed peoples in the world. That being the case, struggle is the natural way to coexistence based on mutual. respect. That vision of the future will come about when the land is created anew in accord with Communist doctrine, what Samiḥ al-Qāsim calls the new Book of Genesis.[37] The struggle of oppressed peoples is personified in the image of Lenin, which passes from one line of fire to another.[38] The goals will be attained only when the red flag is hoisted throughout the world.[39] The victory of the Vietnamese over the Americans was a good omen, and therefore Sālim Jubrān turns to his people and urges them to emulate the Vietnamese.[40] As a sign of identification with the people's struggle throughout the world, these poets address themselves to national liberation movements and national heroes such as the Vietcong rebels, the struggle of the Blacks in America, Lumumba in Africa and Castro in Cuba, Uri Davis and others.

While this group of writers can be clearly classified, the other writers do not divide up into defined groups. They are nationalist writers running the gamut from moderate to radical. When there is movement among them from one stance to another, it is from moderate to radical and not the other way around. Still, it should be noted that despite their harsh criticism expressed in scathing

---

37   Idem, *al-Barākīn*, p. 108.
38   Idem, *al-Mawt al-Kabīr*, p. 50.
39   Tawfiq Zayyād, *Ashud 'Alā Ayādīkum*, pp. 9–11.
40   Sālim Jubrān, *Refaq al-Shams*, Nazareth, 1975, p. 90.

tones, most of the Arab writers in Israel are moderates compared to those in the group called Abnā' al-balad — or the Villagers. The literature of the latter group reflects views basically identical to those of the "rejectionist front" in the Arab world. The representatives of this group — which previously had very few — are Ali al-Sih of the village of 'Arābah in the Galilee, who was mentioned earlier, and Ahmed Hussein from the village of Mousmous in the Triangle. Al-Sih has published two collections of poetry — *Kul Āadhār wa-Antum bi-Khayr** in 1977 and *al-Kitāba bil-Nār*** in 1978. The first collection was published in March 1977 on the anniversary of Land Day in 1976, hence the collection's title. Containing little real poetry, it abounds in sharply worded proclamations. The events of Land Day, as the poet says, brought down the pillars of fear and highlighted the conqueror's weakness, and therefore . . .

> The tongues of rejection have reared
> I reject you
> I will oppose you with my eyes
> I will fight you with my own hands
> For the joy of the land has taught me
> All the ways of violence.[41]

The events of Land Day moved the poet to join the advocates of "rejectionism" — as can be seen from his remarks.[42] Rejectionism is in fact the leitmotif of the second collection, called *Writing with Fire*. The poet opens the collection with a poem he has entitled "Verses from the Sura on Rejection," which calls to mind the Koran, with its verses and suras. Al-Sih holds rejection to be holy, like the Koranic verses. The rejection he advocates seems even more extreme than the position of the

---

* Best Wishes Every March.
** Writing with Fire.
41 Ali al-Sih, *Kul Ādhār wa-Antum bi-Khayr*, pp. 21–22.
42 *Ibid.*, p. 48.

Rejectionist Front countries. He denounces the leaders of the
rejectionist countries for their silence at the time of the attacks
against the Palestinians and leftist forces in Lebanon. He, of
course, also includes the leaders of the oil-rich countries. Here
are several lines as a sampling:

> I am a Palestinian and Fatah represents me
> I crawled while my fire raged ahead of me;
> A suicide-fighter, with rejection dripping from my lips!
> I will attack the bridge and cross over,
> I will wage my battle on the walls of Jerusalem.[43]

Ahmed Hussein, who is also part of the *Abna' al-balad* group,
published two collections of poetry and a book of short stories
between 1977 and 1979. In these works Ahmed Hussein rejects
everything, and focuses only on Palestine and on the Palestinian
cause. He speaks of the Palestinians' struggle, of the bitter life
they lead, and of the plots woven around them by the leaders of
the Arab countries and by foreign forces. Kissinger's efforts to
bring about peace between Israel and Egypt are only a scheme
to guarantee American control of the region and the flow of oil
to the West.[44] It is apparent from this that the poet opposes the
Camp David accords between Israel and Egypt and regards
them as a betrayal of the Palestinian cause. Not only Egypt has
betrayed them, so have all the Arab leaders.[45] Ahmed Hussein's
views are expressed in a sharp, often brutal, way; nevertheless,
he is a writer of stature among his peers in Israel, and, as
I noted, he writes short stories in addition to poetry, and that
gives him a broader readership.

In summary, it can be said that this literature speaks of views
and feelings which are an important but not exclusive element
in determining identity or identification. In a study re-

---

43   Ali al-Siḥ, *al-Kitāba bil-Nār*, 1978, p. 64.
44   Ahmed Hussein, *Zaman al-Khawf*, 1977, pp. 92–93.
45   Ahmed Hussein, *Tarnīmat al-Rab al-Muntaẓar*, 1978, p. 51.

ported not long ago in the Arabic press, Mordecai Avitzur asserted that the Arabs' participation in the life of the country in the economic and social realms is expanding. Sammy Smooha called this phenomenon "Israelization," or a certain measure of identification with Israel in specific realms. Actually, the utilization of freedom of speech to express ideas that are unpopular with the establishment in Israel, or to level harsh criticism against the government, in themselves reflect a measure of Israelization, in the sense of full identification with the country's democratic values. There can be no doubt that a change for the better in the political atmosphere of the region, and especially in the relations between the Jewish people and the Palestinian people, will reinforce this component of the identity of the Arab in Israel. On this point the split in the soul of the Arab in Israel, of which we spoke at the beginning of this review, does in fact appear to exist, and the challenge confronting us is how to overcome this rift between the world of feeling and views and the world of reality — the daily contact with and material attachment to Israeli institutions. And finally, it should be mentioned that everything said above refers to Arab writers as a whole — Moslems, Christians, Druze. The various literary works deal with general problems; differences in approach or treatment stemming from religious community affiliation will not be found in this literature.

46   See *Al-Anbah*, November 30, 1979, p. 7.

ON THE POLITICAL IDENTITY OF THE EDUCATED ARABS IN ISRAEL

MAHMOUD MIARI

In Israel (not including the occupied territories) there are more than 500,000 Arabs, who constitute 14% of the total population. In 1947, these Arabs comprised an integral part of the Arab majority in Palestine (68%) and in the territory on which Israel was established a year later (56%). Officially, the Arabs in Israel are recognized as a minority with "religious and cultural uniqueness." Actually, they are a national minority which shares a common national origin, language and culture with the Arab world in general and the Palestinian people in particular. This national minority is unique, as attested by certain characteristics which are not found together — as far as I know — in any other ethnic minority in the world.

a. *A Colonized Minority.* In their country, the Arabs in Israel constitute a colonized minority dominated by a Jewish majority of immigrants or sons of immigrants. This situation is similar to that of the American Indians in the United States of America.

b. *A Minority Which Participates in the Regional Majority.* Since the Arabs in Israel are a part of the Arab world, they participate in the majority of the wider region, in which the Jewish majority of Israel becomes a small minority.

c. *A Minority Caught Between Groups in Conflict.* The Arabs in Israel are citizens of a state which is at war with their people, the Palestinians, and with their nation, the Arab world. This complex situation, in which the Arabs in Israel are perceived as a "hostile minority," is somewhat similar to that of the Japanese Americans during World War II.

The war of 1948 severed the direct contact and interaction of the Arabs in Israel with the other Palestinians and with the Arab world in general. This situation of severed contact prevailed up to the Six-Day War of 1967, in which the West Bank and the Gaza Strip were occupied by Israel. Seeking to define the political identity of the Arabs in Israel, a research project conducted before and after the Six-Day War revealed that before the war Israel's Arabs identified themselves Israeli, Israeli-Arab, Arab and Palestinian, in that order. The order of identification changed after the war to Arab, Israeli-Arab, Palestinian and Israeli.[1] Defeat in the war and the direct contact of the Arabs in Israel with the other Palestinians strengthened their Arab and Palestinian identifications. In recent years, especially after the October War of 1973, the Palestinian identity has been gaining steadily more ground among the Arabs in Israel. The study, some of the findings of which we shall report below, confirms this development.

The Arabs in Israel were cut off from their old intelligentsia, which left the country in 1948. Over time a small, young intelligentsia developed, trained mostly in the Israeli educational system. In 1974, there were about 1240 university graduates among the Arabs in Israel, not including 600 graduates in East Jerusalem, compared to about 354 graduates in 1961.[2] My study,

---

1 Y. Peres and N. Yuval-Davis, "Some Observations on the National Identity of the Israeli Arabs," *Human Relations* 22 (1969), 219–233.
2 Israel Central Bureau of Statistics, *Statistical Monthly 4* (1977), 37–40.

which was conducted at the Israel Institute of Applied Social Research in Jerusalem, is based on this young intelligentsia. A structured questionnaire was distributed by hand to a sample of about 300 Arab graduates who were asked to answer the questions. A week later the questionnaires were collected by hand. Distribution and collection of the questionnaire were done mostly by the researcher himself. The data were collected between February and July 1976. Some of the findings concerning the political identity of the educated Arabs and their readiness for social relations with Jews are presented below.

The following "national" identities were examined: Israeli, Israeli-Arab, Palestinian and Arab. These identities were measured by the following questions:

To what extent do you feel you are Israeli?
To what extent do you feel you are Israeli-Arab?
To what extent do you feel you are Arab?
To what extent do you feel you are Palestinian?

For each question, the respondents were asked to choose one answer from a range of five categories. The findings show that 91% of the respondents felt "to a very great extent" or "to a great extent" they were Arabs; 76% felt they were Palestinians; 42% felt they were Israeli-Arabs and only 23% felt they were Israelis. If we exclude the Arab identity, about which there is some degree of tolerance by the Jewish majority and the Israeli government, we see that the order of identities that existed before the Six-Day War — Israeli, Israeli-Arab, Arab and Palestinian — has been completely reversed and has become Palestinian. Israeli-Arab and Israeli. In other words, Arab and Palestinian identities are much stronger than Israeli and Arab-Israeli identities.

As expected, a strong positive relationship was found between Israeli and Israeli-Arab identities. This means, generally speaking, that whoever feels he is an Israeli also feels he is an Israeli Arab. A strong positive relationship was also found between Palestinian and Arab identities. An interesting finding was that

Israeli and Arab-Israeli identities were not correlated significantly with Arab identity, but were correlated negatively with Palestinian identity. Generally speaking, an educated Arab who feels he is an Israeli or Israeli-Arab does not feel he is a Palestinian. The reverse is also true: whoever feels he is a Palestinian does not feel he is an Israeli or Israeli-Arab. This finding may be explained by the relation of each identity to the existing political situation: Israeli and Israeli-Arab identities accept the political status quo, while Palestinian identity aims to change it. Since Arab identity coexists with other national identities (such as Egyptian-Arab, Palestinian-Arab, Israeli-Arab, etc.), it seems that this identity has a "moderate" attitude toward status quo.

In addition to the "national" identities mentioned above, the following traditional identities were also examined: religious identity (feeling belongingness to religion), clan identity (feeling belongingness to the hamula) and local identity (feeling belongingness to place of residence). The findings showed that 53% of the respondents felt "to a very great extent" or "to a great extent" that they belong to their place of residence; 29% felt that they belong to their religion; and only 13% felt they belong to their clan (hamula). Strong positive relationships were found among these identities. In other words, if a respondent identifies with one traditional group he tends to identify with other traditional groups as well.

With regard to the relationships between traditional identities on the one hand and "national" identities on the other, it was found that traditional identities were correlated positively with Israeli and Israeli-Arab identities, not correlated significantly with Arab identity and correlated negatively with Palestinian identity. Thus those who define themselves as Israeli or Israeli Arabs tend to be traditional, while those who define themselves as Palestinians tend to be modern.

Let us turn briefly to the educated Arabs' readiness for social relations with Jews and their assessment of Jews' readiness for social relations with Arabs like themselves. This was measured by readiness to work in the same office, to become friendly and to live in the same neighborhood. The asymmetry in Arab-Jewish relations, which Peres[3] and Hoffman[4] reported in their findings, is confirmed and underscored in this study. It was found that Arabs' readiness for social relations with Jews is much greater than their assessment of Jews' readiness for social relations with Arabs like themselves: 86% of the respondents are ready to work in the same office with Jews, as opposed to 16% who assess that Jews are ready to work in the same office with Arabs; 83% are ready to become friendly with Jews, as opposed to 11%, who assess that Jews are ready to become friendly with Arabs; 67% are ready to live in the same neighborhood with Jews, as opposed to 4% who assess that Jews are ready to live in the same neighborhood with Arabs like themselves.

Finally, a few words about the correlation between the respondents' "national" identities and their readiness for social relations with Jews and their assessment of Jews' readiness for social relations with Arabs. The findings show that educated Arabs who identify themselves as Israeli or Israeli-Arab tend more than others to be ready for social relations with Jews and to assess that Jews are ready for social relations with Arabs like themselves. The asymmetry in Arab-Jewish relations, which we discussed earlier, is more frequent among educated Arabs who identify themselves as Palestinian. Their readiness for social relations with Jews is much greater than their perception of Jews' readiness for social relations with them. The Arabs who identify as Palestinian assess more than others that Jews reject social relations with Arabs like themselves.

3 Y. Peres, "Ethnic Relations in Israel," *American Journal of Sociology* 76 (1971), 6.
4 J. Hoffman, "Readiness for Social Relations between Arabs and Jews in Israel," *Journal of Conflict Resolution* 16 (1972), 2.

ARABS IN ISRAEL:
THE SURGE OF A NEW IDENTITY

RAFI ISRAELI

I

Israelis and others are repeatedly stunned by recurring manifestations of self-identity among the Arab minority of Israel.
These outbursts, which express rejection of the Israeli domination
no less than a positive search for identity, have been epitomized
by nationalistic ("we are part of the Palestinian people"), or
irredentist ("we shall liberate you O Galilee!") or religious ("long
live Khomeini!") slogans. On closer examination however, one
should hardly be surprised at these developments, if one considers
the wider context of the rise of Palestinian nationalism and
Islamic revivalism and the concurrent deterioration of Israel's
image and international stature.

By the same token, many Israelis and others have been clinging
to some examples of Arabs who have become established enough
and interested enough to find a place within the Israeli system,
to draw the unwarranted conclusion that Arabs in Israel can be
"Israeli Arabs," as if this were not a contradiction in terms. The
wishful thinking which accompanies the vision of a liberal democratic Israel where the Arab minority can achieve parity with
the Jewish majority, simply runs counter to the fact that most
Arabs in Israel cannot be true Israelis.

Many Israelis and others have been talking of late about the
process of "radicalization" that has taken place among the Arabs
in Israel. By "radicalization" they mean the claims for "national
rights" that are being advanced by this population. It seems to
me, however, that what is termed "radicalization" is actually no
more than a return to the norm; a more emphatic demand that
constant, though hitherto latent, cravings be fulfilled; a surging
self-confidence which is fed by the contemporaneous all-Islamic
success-story; a new outburst of self-righteousness, which presses
for the realization, here and now, of the all-Arab dream of over-
whelming the Jewish polity. Thus, the question of the Arab
minority in Israel, which has grown more acute in recent years,
has truly become a concern for all Israelis, an Israeli problem,
a Jewish-majority problem, no less than an Arab one. The matter
is no longer only one of arm chair morality and of Friday-night
"salon" discussions, but one that touches upon the vitality of the
Zionist idea, the future structure and functioning of Israeli society, perhaps the very existence of the Jewish state. Therefore,
it is incumbent upon anyone who seeks a solution to this sensitive
issue, to not only diagnose its explosive nature but also to
prescribe a way out of the deadlock. For it is no longer plausible
to plaster over the deep gulf separating Jews and Arabs in Israel
or to strive to "buy time" or to slow the inevitable journey down
the collision course; it has become imperative to either bridge the
gap between the two communities, or set them apart to allow for
their mutually tolerant but separate national fulfillment and
development.

II

Among the more than half-a-million Arabs now dwelling in Israel
proper, there seem to prevail four different foci of identity: Israeli,
Palestinian, Arab and Islamic. These foci are not necessarily
always exclusive of each other; rather, the constant search for
identity among the Arabs in Israel seems to have crystalized
into an "incremental" compound whereby they are both "Israeli

and Arab," "Palestinian and Muslim" or any other combination thereof. They seem never to be willing to wear a single tag, always embracing two or more choices, sometimes emphasizing the one, at times insisting upon the other. Four concentric circles may illustrate this dilemma at its highest: the Israeli, the Palestinian, the Arab and the Muslim.

The innermost circle is the Israeli. Ever since the 1948 war, a minority of Arabs has opted to remain under Israeli rule rather than to gain the status of refugee in a neighboring Arab country. But due to the continuing conflict between Israel and its Arab neighbors, Arabs in the Jewish state soon realized that they were torn between their country (Israel) whose citizenship they possessed and whose rights and laws they enjoyed, and their people across the border, who continued to exhort them to shed their loyalty to hateful Israel and actively subscribe to its demolition.

Until the 1967 war, which generated a profound soul-searching among the Arabs, as a result of what some of them bitterly termed their "glorious defeat," the Arabs in Israel were well on their way to accept the idea of the Jewish state and to adjust to their existence as a minority within its confines. Even after the trauma of the Six-Day War, the growth of the Arab minority in Israel was not impeded despite the increasing dilemma inherent in the insolubility of the contradiction between rising national strivings among the Palestinians on the one hand, and Israel's Zionist aspirations on the other.

Indeed, one out of every six Israelis identifies himself as Arab. Among the close to 600,000 Arabs of Israel, 77% are Muslim, 15% Christian and 8% Druze. 47% of this population is concentrated in the North, some 19% in the Jerusalem area, 16% in the Haifa District, and the remainder in the Tel-Aviv and Southern Districts. This population is undergoing a process of urbanization as' evinced in the higher proportion of city-dwellers (some 60%). It is also considerably younger than its Jewish counterpart (average age 20.7 years, compared with 30.4 in the Jewish sector). About 50% of all Arabs in Israel are

14 years old or under, and this is an indication of the vast potential demographic changes that will develop if the Jewish population remains at its present growth rate. The continued improvement of health services in Israel, and the rising standard of living have made their impact on the life expectancy of the Arab population. In the late 1970s, every Arab newborn in Israel had a life expectancy of 63 years (71.5 for females), compared to 64 in Lebanon (before the Civil War), 56 in Syria and Jordan, 55 in Egypt and 45 in Saudi Arabia.

The impressive growth of the Arab community in Israel, from a poor peasant society whose leaders had deserted her in 1948, into a predominantly urban and modern society, is in itself an indication of the pace of acculturation of this minority into the Israeli system. 95% of all school age Arab children attend school at present; in all, 185,000 Arab students attend all levels of schooling within the Israeli system, from kindergarten to university. The younger generation of Arabs who were born and raised within the Jewish state, has produced a new elite of several thousand university graduates and professionals. Moreover, this elite was trained, like the rest of the population, to vote and run for office. At present, in addition to the two Arab municipalities which existed in Israel in 1948, there are some 50 newly established local councils, duly elected by Arab constituencies. Moreover, the process of urbanization notwithstanding, the cultivated area in the Arab villages has grown 2.6-fold since the establishment of Israel, and part of the land is under irrigation and yielding good crops thanks to the mechanization and modern agricultural techniques developed in Israel.

While in 1950 more than half of Arab manpower was employed in agriculture, in the late 1970s only 16% depended on farming for their livelihood, despite the great increase of cultivated areas and productivity. The balance of manpower turned to typically urban occupations such as construction, services, industry and other branches of the economy. By 1976, only half the manpower of the Arab sector was employed locally, while the remainder sought and obtained work outside their localities. The impact on the Arab village has been tremendous: a great boom in construction, modern furnishing, home appliances, roads, electricity, running water, telephones, health and education services, and banks. By the mid–1970s, the Arab population had achieved a higher rate of income per family than Jewish families originating from Asia and Africa, and only slightly lower than the overall Israeli average.

This seemingly smooth integration of the Arab community into Israeli society was nevertheless marked by a growing sense of alienation on the part of individual Arabs. The "liberal" policy of the government, which was devised and implemented through the office of the Prime Minister's Advisor for Arab Affairs, far from contributing to the integration of the Arabs into Israeli society, perpetuated the gap between them. For example, a separate Arab educational system militated against the inculcation of Israeli values into the Arab population. The fact that the Arabs enjoy civil rights, such as the right to vote and to be elected, does not alleviate in the least their frustration at their inability to obtain full acceptance into the Israeli bureaucratic and political elites. A built-in "Catch 22" has developed, whereby the more "liberal" the Israeli policy towards its Arab citizenry, the more vocal have become the demands and the protests of the products of that "liberalism." More and more Arab youths who were educated in Israel, rise against what they view as discriminatory attitudes and policies of the Israeli government. One of them stated in a recent public symposium: "Now that we have attained full material satisfaction, it is time for us to seek spiritual fulfillment."

"Spiritual fulfillment" brings us to the second circle — the Palestinians. Indeed, since the 1967 war, two new developments have dramatically left their imprint on the Arabs in Israel: the rise of Palestinian nationalism and the encounter between erstwhile "Israeli Arabs" and their compatriots in the administered territories of the West Bank and Gaza. Alienated Arabs in Israel seized upon the Palestinian organizations as an outlet for their frustrations and many of them seized every opportunity to state in no uncertain terms their sympathy, if not actual affiliation, with these groups.

When, in March 1976, the Land Day was declared by Arabs in the Galilee as a protest against what they regarded as expropriation of their land, political agitation ensued and irredentist slogans vowing to "liberate the Galilee" from Israel were heard. This outburst, which resulted in loss of life, was accompanied by concurrent wide-scale demonstrations in the cities of the West Bank, in support of their "oppressed brethren" in Israel proper. These combined disturbances were hailed throughout the Arab world as an "uprising of the Palestinian people," on both sides of Israel's pre-1967 borders, against "Israeli occupation."

This open ideological linkage between Israeli Arabs and the Arabs in the administered territories has been one of the most dramatic developments since 1976. Although there had been affinities and emotional ties between the two populations prior to 1976, Land Day manifested the implicit and latent common destiny that the two branches of the same people carried in their hearts.

This does not mean that all Arabs in Israel now necessarily side with the PLO. However, increasing numbers of the Arab youth in the Jewish state, either under the impact of the trauma of the Yom Kippur War, or due to the Palestinian awakening in the administered territories and on the world stage, are now more inclined than ever before to throw in their lot with their compatriots across the "Green Line," under the unifying umbrella of "free, secular and democratic Palestine."

These trends became manifest in the elections of 1976 in the West Bank and the Israeli elections of 1977. In the former, a new and young local leadership arose, which swept aside the traditional patriarchal leadership, and announced its sympathy, if not its formal adherence, to the PLO. During the 1977 Israeli elections, pro-PLO elements either gave their votes to the Communist Rakah Party, or altogether boycotted the elections, as Rakah seemed too moderate for their tastes and not nationalist enough to reflect the mood of the times. Thus, while in the previous elections (1973) some 80% of the Arabs in Israel cast their vote, this time only about 72% went to the polls, the balance being attributed to the boycott by extremist elements. Rakah won more votes than in the previous elections, nearly enough to win them a sixth seat in the Knesset.

The surging Palestinian identity, that many Arabs in Israel now embrace and even proclaim, has made the compound "Israeli-Arab" a contradiction in terms. For not only has the Israeli-Palestinian conflict made it intolerable for the Arabs in Israel to identify as Israelis, but even on the symbolic level the common grounds of Arabs and Israelis have shrunk considerably. Since the Israeli colors symbolize for the Arabs in Israel oppression, expropriation and occupation, the latter naturally prefer the Palestinian flag as their national symbol. Israel Independence Day, which is the most popular festival in Israel, is remembered by the Arabs in Israel as a day of disaster and national humiliation. What is left, then, to build upon as a common denominator for joint nationhood?

No wonder that separatistic trends are noticeable within the Arab community in Israel. Although for the time being separatism can only be expressed culturally (Palestinian literature, a separate system of education, the cultivation of Palestinian-Arab values and heritage and the like), it is evident that the long-term goal is an overthrow of the Zionist state and reunion with other Palestinians. Palestinian nationalism, which has become more or less predominant among Arabs in Israel is the best evidence that nationalistic sentiment does not need to be recognized in order to exist. Whether Israel likes it or not, admits it or not, it is there. All Israel can do is to devise ways of self-defense against this rising nationalism, but she can no longer ignore or deny it.

Then comes the third circle — the Arab. Recent surveys have shown that Arabs in Israel consider themselves Arab no less than Palestinian. In fact, the Palestinian nexus is for them the link to the Arab world, apart from the fact that they share with the rest of the Arabs their language, patrimony, customs and religion. Even "renegade" Sadat attests to the fact that "Palestine is the core of the Arab-Israeli conflict" hence the indissoluble link between being Palestinian and Arab.

If until 1967 Arabs in Israel were deprecated as "collaborators" by many Arab outsiders, their image and worth as potential allies of the Arab world in the war against Israel has been on the rise ever since. Although Arab summons to the Israeli Arabs to revolt against their authorities during the Yom Kippur War went unheeded, Arab propaganda channels never relented in their hope to reverse this situation. During the 1976 events related to Land Day, all Arab leaders, including Sadat, acclaimed "the Arab heroic stand within occupied Palestine," and this certainly added to the Israeli-Arab aura of an all-Arab national struggle against Israel. Moreover, Zionism being in Arab eyes antithetical to Arab nationalism, the Arabs in Israel, whose national loyalty to their people is now beyond doubt, stand in the front line of the all-Arab effort to overwhelm the Zionist polity.

Sadat's peace initiative of 1977 and the ensuing Camp David and peace accords have further complicated the dilemmas of the Arabs in Israel. On the one hand suspicion, skepticism and sometimes hostility were evinced by the Palestinian public towards Sadat, whose dramatic move caused consternation in the rejection front in general and within the Palestinian establishment in particular; but on the other hand, new hopes seemed to glitter for some Palestinians who not only hurried to meet with Sadat during his visit to Jerusalem, but also continued to dispatch successive delegations to Cairo, both to voice their support for his bold initiative and to elicit his pledge that their cause would not be eroded in the process. These delegations represented various strata of Palestinians from the West Bank and

Gaza, although the mayors who are on record as the staunchest proponents of the PLO have obviously and wisely refrained from joining them. The elements of uncertainty which have raised question marks over the applicability of the Camp David agreements to the Palestinian problem, have not diminished after peace was signed between Israel and Egypt and the Autonomy talks were started. Some Arabs in Israel hope to see a new turn of events as a result of peace while others reject the accords, in concert with the Rejection Front, as inadequate as far as the Palestinians are concerned.

The outermost circle is the Islamic one, which has lately gained prominence and world attention due to the Muslim awakening around the globe. Most Arabs in Israel being Muslim, the resurgence of Islam has left its imprint on, and lent an added dimension to, an already difficult situation. Here too, the fact that peace was signed between Israel and one major Muslim country — Egypt — only brought into focus the gap separating Israel and the Jews from Muslims and the Islamic world. President Sadat and his entourage may have overcome the psychological hurdle and recognized the right of existence of the Jewish state, but many Egyptians, and more so other Muslim countries, remain adamant about the rejection of an independent Jewish polity.

In fact, the rejectionists within Egypt, such as the Muslim Brotherhood who openly criticize the peace accords on Islamic grounds, and Deputy Prime Minister Hasan Tuhami who has recently vowed that 2 million Muslims would march on Jerusalem to liberate it, represent the worldwide Muslim norm. Sadat and his party are the exception. Israeli Muslims are part of the world Islamic consensus in this regard, insofar as they sense a five-way grievance meted out to them by Israel:

Firstly, Israel is the home of the Jews, the Qur'anic "wretched people" who are obviously not a nation and therefore do not deserve nationhood. The Jewish claim to a separate political entity constitutes, then, an affront, as it were, to the holy tradition of Islam. Incidentally, this line of argument is echoed in the Palestinian Covenant.

Secondly, the fact that Jews from Arab lands have sought refuge in Israel defies and casts doubt on the Arab-Muslim assertion that the Jews had always benefited from equality and benevolence under Islamic rule. The massive exodus of Jews from those lands and their flow to Israel, belie Muslim contentions as to the fair treatment of the *dhimmis* in their midst. Hence the recurring invitation of Muslim countries to "their" Jews to go back to their original homes, a notion also hinted at in the Palestinian Covenant.

Thirdly, those same Jews who had been condemned to "humiliation and misery," in the holy writings of Islam, have succeeded, though vastly outnumbered, in defeating once and again, the "elected nation of Allah." The Muslims, not least of all the Palestinians, regard this as a travesty of history which has to be redressed.

Fourthly, Israel had been, almost uninterruptedly, part of the Abode of Islam since the 7th century, except for the brief interregnum of the Crusaders. Thus, establishing a non-Muslim state in this part of the world amounts to usurpation of Muslim land. This act of "robbery" performed on the "holy land" of Muslims is therefore likened to the Crusaders' Jerusalem kingdom of the Middle Ages. According to the "logic of history" Israel is, in consequence, bound to be as ephemeral as the Crusader state. A *Jihad* (Holy War) remains, as had been the case in the Middle Ages, the only way to retrieve the lost territories from the "foreign Zionist invaders" who have taken root in Palestine.

Fifthly, if Palestine and other Arab territories are regarded as sacred because they constitute part of the Muslim patrimony, Jerusalem is all the more so, like the pearl in the Islamic crown, due to its link to Muhammad's biography and to subsequent Islamic history.

These basic themes, which are shared, in varying forms and intensities, by many Muslims across the globe, have a direct bearing on the life of Palestinian Muslims. Thus, even more than other Muslims who may feel resentment and frustration at their inability to reverse the situation, the Muslims living under Israeli rule sense the humiliation of being dominated by an erstwhile *dhimmi* people with questionable status in Islamic tradition.

The current revival of Islam has further exacerbated the anti-Israel sentiment among Muslims. The alliance between the Arabs and Khomeini has produced a turn of events whereby the Arab-Israeli conflict has become further Islamized, thus drawing into daily and actual involvement in it Iranian Muslims, not only Arabs (e.g. the recent arrival of a contingent of Iranian "volunteers" into southern Lebanon). Arafat's battle-cry in Teheran "today Teheran, tomorrow Tel-Aviv," coupled with public embraces with Khomeini, more than illustrate this point.

In Israel, as well as in the administered territories, more mosques are being erected than ever before; more and more hitherto alienated youth find their way back to Islam; a group of Muslim sheikhs has been pressing for the establishment of an Islamic college in Israel; and mystical Muslim orders report a soaring membership. In January, 1980, a riot at the biggest Arab village in Israel, Umm-al-Fahm, was reportedly dominated by cries: "Khomeini, Khomeini!" Similarly, in the West Bank and Gaza, Islam has become a refuge for the frustrated Arabs who refuse to live under Israeli occupation. The Muslim leadership in the territories has been cultivating the virtue of persistence *(sabr)* in the face of adverse conditions, and occasionally inciting a "spiritual jihad" as a panacea. In January 1979 a leaflet was distributed in Nablus urging the Believers to "join the great Islamic Revolution that has been taking place in other lands of Islam"; and in January, 1980, disturbances incited by the Muslim Brotherhood wreaked havoc in the offices of the Red Crescent in the Gaza Strip.

The return to Islam does not necessarily mean, however, a daily and scrupulous execution of the tenets of the faith, although this is often the case. In the context of the Muslims in Israel, as elsewhere, Islam has become a focus of identity, a refuge and a shield from the frustrations occasioned by the disappointment with modernization and Westernization. Israel being identified with the West, rising against it and denouncing it also serve the purpose of denying modernity and its Western sources. Moreover, since in recent years the combination of revolution and Islam has become acceptable (Libya, Iran), it has now become possible to support the Palestinian revolution (the "spearhead of the Arab revolution") while at the same time identifying as a Muslim. This is all the more so because being a devoted Muslim and a revolutionary Palestinian serve the same anti-Israeli purpose.

The Islamization of the conflict has lent an international and intercontinental dimension to the Palestinian-Arab problem. Since institution of the Islamic Conference in 1969, which was initially convened under the impetus of the arson attempt on the Al-Aqsa Mosque (August, 1969), all the resolutions of that annual gathering have focused on the questions of Palestine and Jerusalem. Most recently, the Islamabad Conference of Islamic Foreign Ministers (January 1980), which was ostensibly called into emergency session to discuss the Soviet invasion of Afghanistan, ended by condemning Sadat and his peace policy and reaffirming the rejectionist all-Islamic consensus. Such a stance, adopted by representatives of 700 million Muslims, cannot but encourage Palestinian Arabs/Muslims, including those residing in Israel, in their negative attitudes towards a peaceful settlement with the Zionist state.

The superpower scramble to placate and please the Muslims, following recent events in Iran and Afghanistan, only add to the sentiment of self-confidence and self-righteousness of the Islamic world in general and the Palestinian-Arab-Muslims in particular. If the world is courting them; if the Americans are hinting at the need to solve their problem, at the expense of Israel if necessary; if the European Community is attempting to amend Resolution 242 so as to recognize their national aspirations; what incentive do the Palestinian Arabs, and Israeli Arabs among them, have to rush to a compromise? The feeling prevails in their quarters, that if they wait long enough and endure consistently enough, they will have their way by the sheer presence and power of the international Muslim community.

III

In the light (or rather obscurity) of the above analysis one is bound to abandon any hope of a workable solution or at least a *modus vivendi* and *modus operandi* between Israel and the Palestinian Arabs living in its midst. To avoid over-simplification, however, it is necessary to isolate certain elements which may be conducive to a partial settlement of this seemingly insoluble problem.

Recent surveys have shown that about 20% of the Arab population in Israel have become reconciled to the idea of an independent Jewish-Zionist state, and to the prospect of continuing to live as a cultural minority in such a polity. The remainder of the Arab population in Israel, that is the majority, has voiced varying degrees of identification with Palestinian or Arab nationalism, and has thereby, explicitly or implicitly, denounced the existence of a Zionist Israel as a separate political entity. The practical implication of this cleavage is that the minority group of 20% regards itself as Israeli and is apparently prepared to bear the consequences of its alignment, the majority of 80% would rather use the claim to Israeli citizenship only as a matter of convenience, in order to legitimize its demands for equality and rights. In other words, the minority seems to be prepared to pay the price of its attachment to Israel, and its corollary detachment from the larger Arab-Palestinian identity, while the majority is only willing to get what it can (equal rights, budgets, development, higher education and the like) and to use what it got in order to further its anti-Israeli goals.

Faced with this situation, Israel must devise a differential treatment to these two populations: to encourage, adopt and integrate the former, and separate, detach itself from the latter. For example, a semi-autonomous Arab educational system in Israel has militated against the inculcation of Israeli values into the Israeli Arab population. The fact that the Arabs enjoy civil rights, such as the right to vote, but are exempt from national duties, such as military service, has created two societies in Israel: Jewish "insiders" and Arab "outsiders." If the acquisition of Israeli citizenship and of civil rights (by Jews and Arabs alike) could be made contingent upon the fulfillment of one's national duties on the one hand, and if all channels of national promotion in the army and the bureaucracy were open to the conforming Arabs, on the other, conditions would be created for genuine integration.

One must realize, however, that due to the ongoing Arab-Israeli conflict and the national sensitivities involved, most of the Arabs in Israel who now feel more akin to their Palestinian brethren than to their Israeli compatriots, cannot be made to embrace Israeli values. The Arab students' demonstrations on Israeli campuses, their insistence on celebrating their national festivals and brandishing their symbols, and their flat refusal to share the burden of nightwatching in university dormitories where they reside, are only a few manifestations of these sentiments. A positive motivation should, therefore, be created with a view to rewarding and ultimately truly integrating those who wish to join the Israeli-Zionist endeavor. The Arabs who are ready to receive Israeli-Hebrew education, to serve in the military and swear allegiance to the state, should be wholeheartedly and unreservedly welcomed into the Israeli establishment, while those who refuse to do so (and one can understand their reluctance), should remain devoid of such civil rights as voting. Many western democratic countries recognize the status of residents (permanent or temporary) who are not allowed to vote unless they acquire citizenship. Arab residents will not be required to serve in the military or to enrol in the Israeli public educational system, but will not enjoy civil rights such as the right to vote, and will have to provide for their own private education.

The experience of the peoples in other places has shown that it is preferable by far to allow two culturally different groups to maintain separate existences and cultivate good neighborly relations between two proud and independent entities, than to force one upon the other or try to share the power between them on a basis of quotas. This is simply not a workable solution (viz. Cyprus and Lebanon) although it may be appealing, morally and otherwise, and soothing to the ego of visionaries of "friendship and amity between nations." The poor achievements of the many "associations for understanding and friendship between Arabs and Jews" in Israel are the best evidence of their futility.

It is clear that the rise of Palestinian nationalism, coupled with the mounting tide of Islam, have made impossible the continued containment, under Israeli rule, of an Arab political-minded population, as a minority devoid of national rights. If some sort of autonomy or self-rule can be worked out, and accepted, by the Palestinians in the West Bank and Gaza, then the majority of Israeli Arabs, who want to have no part in Zionist Israel, may very well join, at a later phase, "autonomous Palestine," without forfeiting their right of residence in Israel. Incidentally, a similar arrangement is envisaged for the Israeli settlements in the West Bank after autonomy is achieved. Only thus, could a reconciliation and final settlement come about between Israel and its Arab population. However, due to the current stance of the PLO, which insists on "all of Palestine," the prospects for such a mutually agreed solution seem very dim indeed.

Israel has no choice, then, but to enforce, unilaterally, the first part of this program which, if proved workable, would at least show that a solution is in sight for part of the Arabs living in Israel. The rest will be, as a consequence, either motivated to join in the successful experiment, or to prevail upon the rest of the Palestinians to accept autonomy as the only alternative.

Chapter VI

THE ESSENTIAL PROBLEM:
WHAT SHOULD BE THE MUTUAL RELATIONS BETWEEN MAJORITY AND MINORITY IN A JEWISH STATE?

THE ATTITUDE OF JUDAISM
TO MINORITIES

DAVID GLASS

Some preliminary comments. I am not an expert on relations between Jews and Arabs. I will try to deal with Judaism's approach to the issue of majority-minority relations in a Jewish state. Even if the state does not rest on Halakhic foundations, its modes of behavior should be guided by basic Jewish principles.

I add nothing new by saying that there is something unique about Israel's situation, and when dealing with questions of majority confronting minority it must be kept in mind that there are here two circles or frames of reference, one within the other. In the State of Israel there is a Jewish majority and an Arab minority, but in the region as a whole a Jewish minority faces a vast Arab majority, with the Arab minority in the country feeling an attachment to that surrounding population. Visually, our situation can be seen as a pincers of sorts, with the weaker jaw the Arab minority in the country, and the strong, menacing jaw the mostly hostile Arab majority of the countries in the region, with the Jews of the State of Israel located in the middle. The circle is both broadened and drawn tighter when the growing phenomenon of Islamization is taken into account; that too must be considered in any discussion of the question of majority-minority relations in Israel. My dovish political credentials are fairly well known. I needn't present them here; nevertheless, I must admit that I re-examine my world outlook every single day, for it is clear to me and to us all that the smallest error in foreign and defense relations and to our relations with our neighbors is liable to cost us very dear.

There is a view which in its most extreme form is represented by Meir Kahana. For him, every Arab is an actual or potential "fifth columnist"; he therefore concludes that we have to seek to drive out the Arabs of Israel and of the territories at once or in stages. Were Kahana alone in holding this view, it might be possible to be unconcerned about it. But, I am sorry to say, that view has a much broader lodging, including those who express it in closed forums and those who express it in deeds. We need only recall the recent utterances of the army's chief of the Northern Command, or those of the head of the Ministry of the Interior's Northern District that the Arabs in Israel are "a cancer in the body of the land." But the evil issues not only from the north; many others share this view, although at this stage they are keeping it down to a whisper. I am not sure which of them is more dangerous. Not long ago I had the occasion to be in one of the settlements in Judea and Samaria. I don't shrink from such confrontations, but I must admit, that for the first time in my life, I was struck dumb by the first question put to me in that place: "What would you do if you were Joshua and were commanded to destroy the seven peoples?" After a moment of stupefaction, I answered that if I had a choice I'd rather be Isaiah and not Joshua, and then I returned the ball to the questioner's court, asking him what he would do. It was clear to all those present that the question alluded to practical applications in the present; the settlement is in fact surrounded by Arab villages. He replied that in the first stage he would ask the Arabs to leave the country willingly. I asked what he would do if they chose not to leave willingly. He replied: "In that case I would force them to leave." I thought that was one man's view, but to my astonishment I saw that many of those present supported it. There are many people in Israel who think likewise, but do not give public expression to their views. As I said, I don't know who is more dangerous, those shouting at the gate or those poisoning the wells clandestinely.

In my view, such a doctrine is fascist, inhumane, unjust and also politically unwise. It is also in utter opposition to the spirit of Judaism. It is very important to explain Judaism's position with regard to non-Jewish minorities, if only because quite a few observant Jews are contributing to the creation of an erroneous view of the Halakhic outlook on this. Those people clothe their extremist political views in a mantle of Halakhic reasons; they are like an archer who shoots and only afterwards draws circles around the arrows. I will therefore expound the Halakhic attitude towards minorities by citing some of the relevant sources, but what I can offer here is no more than a drop in the vast ocean of Israel's heritage.

The fundamental principle in the Torah on this issue is contained in the verses: "You shall have one statute, both for the stranger and for him that is born in the land" (Numbers 9:14) and "There shall be one statute both for you and for the stranger that sojourns with you, a statute forever throughout your generations; as you are so shall the stranger be before the Lord. One law and one ordinance shall be both for you and for the stranger that sojourns with you." (Numbers 15: 15–16). This does not refer (as might be misconstrued) to someone who has converted and has taken upon himself the yoke of the Jewish religion. Such a stranger *(ger)* is called a *ger tzedek*, while the stranger referred to here is a *ger toshav*, i.e., a person who has accepted Noah's seven commandments, which are the basic rules of human behavior required for the existence of society anywhere. Of him it is said — one statute, one ordinance, one law for you and for him. Maimonides said that a *ger toshav* is spoken of as being "one of the righteous of the nations."

This injunction to treat the *ger toshav* without discrimination

and with full equality of rights is repeated many times in the
Bible and a series of Halakhic rulings were passed based on
it. For example, it is a duty to extend financial aid and support
to a *ger toshav,* as it is written, "and [if] his means fail with
you, then you shall uphold him, as a stranger [*ger*] and settler
[*toshav*] shall he live with you" (Leviticus 25:35). Commenting
on this verse, Rashi says that it refers to the *ger toshav,* "do not
let him fall, for then it is hard to raise him up, but uphold him
when he shows signs of falling." Nachmanides (who often is
cited as the sole justification for the doctrine of the "Greater
Land of Israel") counts this injunction among the 613 *mitzvot.**
In his words, "We are commanded to restore to life the *ger
toshav* and to rescue him from his distress. If he is drowning
in a river or a wave falls on him we are to exert all our strength
to save him; if he is sick, we should busy ourselves with his
healing." He adds, "since we are commanded to restore him to
life, he is to be healed free of charge, and the daughter of a
ger toshav giving birth is to be attended [even] on the Sabbath."
As for where the alien is to live, Maimonides rules, after the verse
"He shall dwell with thee, in the midst of thee, in the place he
shall choose within one of thy gates, where it liketh him best;
thou shalt not wrong him." (Deuteronomy 23:16): "A *ger toshav*
is to be settled where he can earn his livelihood and practice
his faith, as it is written, 'in the place he shall choose'."

For the sake of balance it must be added that Maimonides —
and not he alone — also ruled that as much care as possible
must be taken not to settle the *ger toshav* on the border, so as
not to place him in a moral dilemma should war break out with
the enemy on the other side of the border. According to Maimonides, the very term *ger toshav* (resident alien) indicates that he
can be settled among us in Eretz Israel. The permission to sell
land in Eretz Israel to a *ger toshav* follows from that.

The renowned commentator on the Bible, the Malbim, adds

*   Commandements of the Torah.

some instructive points on this subject. "A *ger toshav* will not be exiled from one city to another; it is written 'within one of thy gates so that the residents of the city living there will not say that he is trespassing; and he is brought from a bad dwelling place to a beautiful one; it is written 'where it liketh him best,' so the alien is to dwell where he can earn his livelihood as the other inhabitants do, and he should be settled in a place that is good for his bodily health, so that it truly 'liketh him best'."

The Jewish Halakhic injunction is, as stated, to treat the non-Jewish minority with absolute justice, without any discrimination. To quote Maimonides once again: "The *ger toshav* is to be treated with respect *(derech eretz)* and benevolence *(gemilut hasadim)*." Elsewhere he says: "It is forbidden to cheat a *ger toshav*." In *Hilchot Melachim*, Maimonides also rules that a minority living among a Jewish majority must be allowed to maintain its own judicial system, and only if it does not do so is a Jewish court provided for it. Such a minority is to be allowed to judge and be judged according to laws and statutes it is accustomed to. He asserts, furthermore, than when a Jew and a *ger toshav* are engaged in a lawsuit, the ruling is not to be done from the side that gives the Jew the edge. The system in which the Jew benefits is not to be sought and instead, "they are always to be judged according to their law." What greatness, what a true sense of justice, honesty and equality before the law is contained in those words!

Beyond the demand for equality and justice, the Torah commands love of the *ger toshav*, as it is written, "And you shall love him like yourself." The Torah commands Israel forty-six times to act towards the *ger toshav* out of love. The explanation for this absolute demand also recurs a number of times: "And thou shalt love him as yourself; for you were strangers in the land of Egypt" (Leviticus 19:34); "And you shall not oppress a stranger; for you know the heart of a stranger, since you were strangers in the land of Egypt" (Exodus 23:9). The author of *Sefer Hachinuch* ("The Book of Education"), Rabbi Aaron Ha-levi, explains the mention of the Exodus from Egypt as the reason for the duty to love the stranger as follows: "For you were strangers in the land of Egypt, reminding us that we were already scorched by the great anguish shared by all who find themselves among strange people in a foreign land. And remembering the great anxiety in that, for we already suffered it, and God in his mercy took us out from there, our compassion is stirred for every man in that situation." Note the profound psychological understanding of the soul of the minority member contained in this explanation. Rabbi Samson Raphael Hirsch, one of the great rabbis of Germany, the advocate of the method in Judaism called "Torah and *derech eretz*," which can be broadly translated as "Law and Civility" — summed up this subject: "For you were strangers in the land of Egypt and experienced firsthand to what cruel harshness a state can descend when it perverts the law against the stranger. The law of your land, therefore, will be rooted in the principle of full equality for all its inhabitants. One statute and one law for the citizen and the stranger. Respect and love for the stranger are the true touchstone of your love and fear of Me." Rabbi Samson Raphael Hirsch warned that unfair behavior towards the stranger leads in the end to the corruption and degeneration of the state itself. Love for the stranger, treating him with tolerance and as an equal, are the touchstones of the first and all-important commandment enjoined upon a Jewish person, namely, the love of God. The love of God is proven by and depends on love for the minorities.

Too many quotations, perhaps, but, as I stressed, I felt duty bound to set things right and to present Judaism's true view of the subject of our discussion. I don't have to search humanistic-liberal doctrines in order to find sources for a humane attitude towards the minorities. It is enough to dip into the treasures of Israel. From those sources we draw genuine pearls of human kindness.

I will add a few general remarks on the subject of majority-minority relations in the country, again from the point of view of someone not an expert on it. I believe that relations between the Jewish majority and the Arab minority should be based on rights and duties on both sides. I would lay down two obligations for the Arab minority: recognition of the sovereignty of the state within boundaries over which there is the broadest national consensus, and recognition and acceptance of the fact that this state is a Jewish and Zionist state, with all that follows from that. The obligations of the Jewish majoriy towards the Arab minority I see as the maintenance of absolute equality of rights not only in theory but also in practice; recognition of the minority's right to preserve and promote its cultural and religious heritage; and genuine integration of members of the Arab minority in all sectors in Israel.

These principles should be anchored in law. The Knesset Constitution and Legal Committee has recently begun to deliberate on a proposed Basic Law — Human Rights. Its paragraph 2 stipulates: "All are equal before the law A person [another version has a 'citizen'] is not to be discriminated against on grounds of race, sex, nationality, ethnic community, origin, religion, outlook, social status or political affiliation, or on any other grounds." It is important that this basic law be adopted soon, one reason being to ensure the rights of the minorities. At the same time, it must be noted once again that legislation, however good it may be, is not the entire solution. One of the finest constitutions in the world in terms of the protection of human rights is that of the Soviet Union. . . . Even if we have the finest constitution that will not suffice. The decisive factor is the social climate in the country, the spirit of tolerance of individuals and groups, even those whose views — even actions — are at odds with those of the majority. That is the hallmark of true democracy.

I would like to conclude with illustrations dealing with the relation not to minority members but to an actual enemy. As is known, the origin of the shofar blasts on Rosh Hashanah and at the close of Yom Kippur — *teqi'ah, shevarim, tru'ah* — is the clamorous lament of the mother of Sisera, according to the verse, "Through the window she looked forth and moaned, the mother of Sisera" (Judges 5:28). Note what situation is described in the Scriptures. Sisera's mother is awaiting the return of her son from battle with the armies of Israel. When the sounds of his chariots are late in coming, she, filled with worry and anxiety, bursts into tears. That sobbing, those mother's tears — even though she is the mother of an enemy of the Jews who wants to destroy Israel — are to this day example and symbol of shofar blasts, one of the most sacred acts of the Jewish people.

A second example, perhaps a bit more relevant to our subject, is the story in Genesis about the boy Ishmael, the son of Abraham, who was driven out together with his mother Hagar. They wandered together in the desert around Beersheba. When the water in the skin-bottle was finished and the child was about to die of thirst, an angel of God appeared to Hagar from heaven, produced a well for her and said: "Fear not, for God has heard the voice of the lad where he is." The Midrash relates that at that time the ministering angels were angry with God and said to him something like the following: The man whose sons and sons' sons will kill your sons by thirst, you raise up a well for him? And God answered: Now what is he, a righteous person or a wicked? They said to Him: A righteous! Right away He rose up a well for him. . . ." I think the moral of this marvelous story is clear.

Since those distant days many generations have come and gone and much blood has been shed in wars between the descendants of Ishmael and the descendants of Isaac. Perhaps the time has finally come for the great reconciliation. I believe it has, and that the minority living among us can and must be a bridge towards that reconciliation whose day is coming.

THE VIEW OF AN ARAB ATTORNEY

ELIAS HOURI

In his article, David Glass* portrays an ideal situation, what ought to be. But, it seems to me, that situation does not exist anywhere in the world — although attempts are made to reach it. I would like to add to Glass' remarks about how Israel's existence is viewed. The first president of the state, Chaim Weizmann, said that the world would judge the State of Israel by how it treats its Arab citizens. As I understand the concept, mutual relations between majority and minority refers to a two-way relationship between two bodies, two peoples living in the same region. This relationship requires the cooperation of both sides, each side giving and each receiving. In this sense, since the establishment of the state there has been no policy that would encourage "mutual relations" between Jews and Arabs in Israel. The relationship has been one-way, and therefore change is necessary. The policy must change in the direction of participation by the Arab minority in policy-making processes and of granting rights along with the obligations that are imposed on this minority. Mutuality in this sense is an important and fundamental element. Both sides must obtain a minimum of satisfaction. This should

* See p. 187.

be expressed in the economic, social and national-religious realms. In the social realm it should be expressed in participation of Arabs in the state systems and organizations in the regions where they live. The persons so participating should be in leadership positions, so as to be able to guide the people they serve.

Mutuality can also be expressed in the educational system. The Arabs can be given the possibility — in areas densely populated by them, the north for example — to plan the regions in which they live. It must also be expressed by the Ministry of Education, by eliminating separate educational systems controlled or directed by Jewish parties whose main concern in Arab education is to induce forgetfulness or perhaps to distract, whose only desire is to prevent the Arab minority from knowing its own background, history and nationality. Today the Arab curriculum does not include Arab history, but has an abundance of classes in Jewish or Zionist history. The office called the "adviser on Arab affairs" must also be abolished. An office of that kind exists only in the State of Israel. It must be abolished for it does not serve the interests of the Arabs. It serves the interests of the Jewish majority.

As for the future, the national aspirations of the minority living in this country must also be taken into account. This minority lives in the setting that surrounds it — a majority of Arab countries around the state. This minority remembers that it once was the majority in this country and then suddenly, as the result of an historical process, the Jewish national awakening, it became a minority deprived of its rights. In every action, in all policy that is drawn up, in all policy that is implemented in the Arab sector, the sensitivity of the Arab minority must be taken into account. This sensitivity stems from the fact that this Arab minority senses a looming danger: the Jewish majority endangers its existence by settling in its regions, by taking without giving, by taking the territory on which the minority resides. That differs from the situation in other parts of the world, where minorities do not face such a danger. When lands are expropriated in the Galilee or elsewhere in the country, lands generally of Arab ownership, that Arab feels pain, feels his rights being violated, therefore he does not cooperate and is unable to see mutuality. He sees that the land taken from him ostensibly for development is taken in order to be given to another, without development of the region for his benefit as well. All bodies and parties connected with this should begin to think about planning for the Arab sector, long-range planning extending also to the expropriated lands, so that the Arabs too will begin to receive plots for public and industrial construction.

I want to stress once again that in all policy decision-making processes, the interests of the Arab minority in Israel must also be taken into account. Development and industrialization must also be for the Arabs. Glass contended that according to the Bible, the source of Hebrew law, the stranger living among you must be given consideration, his rights must not be deprived without giving him anything. Thus, when it is maintained that the Jewish Agency or some other Jewish body overseas helps to develop a particular area where Jews live, that does not mean that the Arabs are not entitled to a part of that development.

Mutuality should also find expression in propaganda and the communications media. The media should highlight the moderate minority among the Arabs, those who recognize the State of Israel's existence and its right to exist within secure boundaries, rather than highlighting the extremists, who make up a small minority within the Arab population. A proper information policy would show the Jewish public what is going on in the Arab sector, so that the two camps could draw closer to each other. For the relationship is not an ideal one but an actual matter of daily behavior by individuals toward one another.

The question of the relationship with the Arabs should be formulated not as "how to treat the Arabs" but as "how to live with the Arabs"; that is what we should expect from the authorities.

"How to live with the Arabs" means a joint life by the two peoples residing in the same place, based on mutual consideration of each other's rights. I said that the Arab minority here differs from other minorities in the world. It differs from the Welsh in Great Britain, the Frisians in the Netherlands and the Basque peoples in Spain. The difference is that those minorities do not see that their existence is endangered. They do not feel that the territory on which they reside might be taken from them, that, for example, among the Basques it will be made Spanish, or among the Frisians it will be made Dutch like the other parts of Holland. In Israel, too, there must be a policy that will convince those Arabs not to feel, as they now do as a consequence of acts in the field, that the lands on which they reside are to be taken from them, that they will be deprived of their rights, that perhaps their very existence on that territory will endanger them.

I do not demand that the relationship be ideal, for I know it is too complicated for that. In this entire process it is important to take into consideration all the factors I have enumerated, for they are part of the society in which we live, part of what the Arabs in the country feel today. Therefore, real change in this direction will be beneficial.

THE VIEW OF A SECULAR JEW

YEHOSHUA PORATH

In his beautiful and penetrating remarks, Anton Shamas used
the expression "the fire threatening us all" to make vivid what
many of us apparently feel — that we are nearing an explosive
situation. The anger and bad feeling the two national groups
have towards each other are such that in a certain situation —
say, war — they may ignite into a great conflagration in which
all of us will suffer as human beings and as civilized people.
We should therefore examine the question of the status of the
Arabs in Israel, the sooner the better, in order to try to arrive
at a diagnosis and to propose at least a partial remedy, in the
hope that it is still possible to work towards a solution of the
problem.

I believe that there are grounds for hope, especially now that
a large and important Arab country has opted for peaceful relations with Israel. I am convinced that a real and effective breach
in the solid wall of Arab hostility towards Israel will blunt the
prevailing stereotype held by the Jews, which has all the Arabs
as hostile to Israel and its Jewish inhabitants, and waiting for
the first opportunity to liquidate the state and wipe out its inhabitants. Fear of universal Arab hostility and the anxiety
evoked by the uniformly negative stance towards Israel taken by

all the Arab countries worsened relations between Jews and Arabs in Israel, which were not very good to begin with. It may also be hoped that peaceful and good neighborly relations with Egypt will put an end to the negative, antisemitic images of the Jews, and especially of the Israelis, prevailing among the Arabs. The importance, for our subject, of the change that has come about in the relations between Israel and Egypt, must be stressed; the new climate that will be established between Israel and Egypt may facilitate the work of those of us who are searching for ways to cool down or maybe even to extinguish, the fire burning in the relations between Jews and Arabs.

This examination is incisive, reaching as it does to the roots of our national identity as Jews and Israelis; it is equally so for the Palestinian Arabs who, after 1948, became citizens of the State of Israel. It seems to me impossible to evade consideration of the cardinal question of identity when dealing with the nature of the relations between Jews and Arabs in Israel. Until now we have trod a path paved by the founders of the state (the validity of which went virtually unchallenged): the State of Israel was established, and must continue to exist, as a Jewish state, as the crowning achievement of the struggle of the Jewish national movement; it is an instrument for the solution of the Jewish question, a response to Jewish distress in the Diaspora, and, with redoubled force, it is a means to relieve the suffering and humiliation of the remnants of the Jewish people after the Holocaust. The Arabs of Israel were caught within this state. Their formal legal equality was accepted by virtually everyone, but at the same time it was apparent and accepted that they could not identify with the state's symbols of identification and collective goals, or regard it as a framework expressive of their collective desires. For humanistic, liberal or socialist reasons, or on the basis of a humanistic interpretation of the Jewish religious tradition, the view that came to be accepted in Israel was that the treatment of the Arabs in Israel must be more or less fair, but that they cannot be a part of the "state's nation":

they are not part of the national collective that identifies with the state, which sees it as a framework for the expression of its national identity and which is prepared to fight for its survival. This was a relatively easy course to follow, for it was acceptable to the vast majority among both of the national groups in the country, and consequently the discussion of this question was shunted aside and deferred. But now we have reached a stage where, unless a new path is marked out, it will be difficult to continue together.

The basic factors that have made the present situation possible are changing before our very eyes. A demographic revolution is taking place among the Arabs of Israel. Hareven* has already noted that since 1967 their annual rate of natural increase has been about 3.7 percent. I should like to point out that a population increasing at that rate doubles itself within 22 years. There is nothing to indicate that in the future this rate will substantially decline. Furthermore, in the early fifties the Arabs of Israel had neither leadership nor intelligentsia. The important Palestinian Arab urban centers were on the other side of the border, while in Haifa and Jaffa only few members of the wealthy and educated strata remained. The Arabs of Israel were for the most part impoverished, uneducated fellahin, or unskilled workers at a low level of organization. On the other hand, there was large-scale Jewish immigration to the country and until 1952 the Arabs' share of the population in Israel declined. Under such circumstances the conception that nothing needs to be demanded of the Arabs other than formal observance of law and public order could gain acceptance. No one demanded that they be actively involved in the life of the country, and no one thought of shaping the values and symbols of the state in such a way that the Arabs of Israel too would be able to identify with them. Nor did anyone demand that they identify with an opposing conception. In the eyes of the Arab

---

* See p. 3.

countries and the Palestinian leaders outside of Israel the Arabs of Israel were then a strange hybrid creature; many of those leaders even regarded them as traitors who preferred the "sweet" life in Israel to the bitter Palestinian fate of refugee life.

That situation is gone, probably never to return. Today the Arabs of Israel number three times what they were at the time of the birth of the state. There has been impressive growth among them of literacy and of secondary and higher education. Their economic activity has diversified considerably, and along with laborers and fellahin one now finds many office workers, teachers, lawyers, journalists, merchants, entrepreneurs, businessmen, etc. Their standard of living has risen absolutely and relatively. They form a public that is seeking to express itself and is in search of symbols of identity and channels of activity. They are no longer satisfied with the personal advancement of their children and are seeking ways to express their collective identity as well. Unlike in the past, the Palestinian leaders on the outside view the Arabs of Israel as an inseparable part of the Palestinian Arab people and call upon them to join its struggle. Today the Arabs of Israel have the tools required for taking that path, if they so choose. With their numbers they have the power to operate within Israel's democratic political system, to influence its moves, perhaps even disrupt it. (Does anyone recall the tremendous influence that Parnell and Redmond's Irish national party had on parliamentary life in Great Britain in the thirty years prior to World War I?) They can create pressure by extra-parliamentary means. Their level of education enables them to utilize the communications media to air their positions, and to educate and consolidate their public; and their income level and economic situation provides a basis for financing all these activities. In my view, if the State of Israel is not prudent enough to present its Arabs with an alternative to the course proposed by the PLO, then those Arabs will gradually take the only course offered them. I have no doubt what option they will take if they have to choose between a national course as proposed by the PLO, and acceptance of political and identi-ficational emasculation, the situation that exists today in Israel (although I am not sure that the alternative course offered by Israel will easily, and in all instances, win out over the PLO nationalist option).

On the other hand, Zionism too has been changing in recent years, taking on a more extremist mien. After 1948, the vast majority of us regarded the establishment of a Jewish state in part of Palestine as satisfying national longings and as meeting the need of building a refuge for that part of the Jewish people requiring it; now, however, the conception taking increasing hold maintains that a state in part of Eretz Israel does not meet Zionism's fundamental objectives and that it is necessary to re-turn to a Greater Land of Israel so that it can serve as a basis (a mystical one, so it seems to me) for the complete return to the Jewish people's spiritual-religious roots. By its very nature, such a process of return-rebirth is not distinguished by tolerance of the views and beliefs of the other, nor is it rooted in a ration-alistic-humanistic conception about freedom of choice and the sovereignty of reason; it bears within it the seeds of a negative attitude towards the members of another people, repelling them, or at least closing them out.

At the same time as this spiritual-ideational process has been taking place, the true substance of Zionism — *aliya*, immigration to the country — has been steadily diminishing. The mass im-migration in the four years following the War of Independence and its continuation on a somewhat smaller scale during the subsequent twenty years were apparently a one-time phenome-non stemming from factors not likely to recur (and best that they do not). After World War II some 300,000 Jewish displaced persons were gathered in Central Europe: survivors of the death camps or those who had hidden in crannies of houses and in the forests of Eastern Europe and who after the war had escaped in the "flight" movement to the displaced persons camps in the areas of the Allies' occupation in Austria, Germany and

Italy. These Jews refused to return to their original lands, but the United States and most of the traditional countries of immigration were closed to them then as they had been before the war. (The United States began to ease its immigration laws related to Jewish refugees only at the end of 1949.) And so, two-thirds of these homeless people made their way to the State of Israel. In the countries of the Eastern Bloc a large Jewish grouping still existed in Rumania (about 500,000 people), there were several hundred thousand Jews in Hungary and about 100,000 Polish Jews who came out of bunkers and hiding places in "Aryan" regions or returned to Poland from the Soviet Union. Most of them did not adjust to the Communist regime: a few tried and failed; many others had been Zionists all along. All these Jews were candidates for immigration to Israel. In the Arab and Moslem countries there were close to a million Jews, who ever since the eruption of the national conflict in Palestine were caught in its crossfire. Quite a large number of them joined up with the Zionist movement and organized a heroic Zionist underground and an underground *aliya* movement (Iraq). Others huddled against the wind, waiting for the storm to pass. But raging with greater fury, it threatened to destroy them, and most of them were forced to leave those lands and immigrate to Israel or to Europe (mainly to France).

That was the basis for the mass immigration and its prolongation for about twenty years. In the last decade this constellation of circumstances has altogether changed and this potential pool for *aliya* has been more or less exhausted. On the other hand, Zionism has never succeeded in bringing about immigration to Israel on a meaningful scale from countries where the Jews were not persecuted, or in which persecution and antisemitism were at a level the Jews regarded as tolerable and with which they felt they could live. Assimilationist processes are very powerful in such countries, and have been for some time. Examining the composition of the Jewish communities in the countries of northern Europe, we find that the largest groups among them are refugees from Eastern Europe who arrived after the Russian Revolution, survivors of World War II, or those disappointed with socialism in the sixties and seventies. Little remains of the Jewish communities formed in the Scandinavian countries in the early nineteenth century; similarly, in England, only a few of the old English Jews, who arrived before the waves of Jewish immigration from Eastern Europe that began at the end of the nineteenth century, are still to be found. Among the Jews of Germany as well the extent of assimilation up until World War I was very great, despite the waves of reaction against the Emancipation that had already surfaced in the period of the Kaiser. Need much be said about the United States, a multi-community country in which the Jews are perceived as one ethnic group among many, and quite well off at that?

The reality of recent years has taught us that even groups of Jews of semi-refugee status are not a potential source of *aliya*. The Jews of Algeria, who left their country together with the Europeans, settled in France. The Jews of Cuba moved to the United States, together with the other Cubans who refused to live under savior Castro's rule. Most of the Jews of Iran, too, accepted life under the enlightened regime of Khomeini rather than leaving their country, and most of those who did decide to leave Iran did not come to Israel.

What happened among the Jews of the Soviet Union is also very significant. As long as most of those leaving the USSR were from the periphery, the majority did in fact come to Israel. The Jews of the Baltic region, Bukovina, Bessarabia and Georgia had apparently preserved the tradition of Jewish identity and Zionist belief, and when they were presented with the opportunity — they went to Israel. Being in the forefront of the trend, they benefited from good material conditions without yet encountering the negative attitude towards new immigrants from the Soviet Union that those conditions evoked. By contrast, the Jews of the Russian and Ukrainian republics and their major cities — Moscow, Leningrad, Odessa, Kiev, etc. — prefer immigration to the West rather than to Israel. These people, most of whom are educated and can be absorbed in the developed countries, are motivated by a desire to escape a totalitarian regime, not by Zionism. The reservoir of Jews of the first type is, however, drying up, except for the concentration in Central Asia of traditional Jews who lack skills suitable for a western labor market. It may be surmised that the Soviet Union too is no longer a potential source of large-scale immigration to Israel.

The inescapable conclusion, therefore, is that since the rate of natural increase of the Arabs of Israel is at least twice that of the Jews of Israel, a day will come when it will be difficult to maintain the character of Israel as a Jewish state by democratic means. When the Arabs of Israel will be a minority comprising 30 percent of the population, it will be impossible to ignore them when considering the nature of the state, the elements of its policy, and its national priorities and symbols, without drastically changing the democratic character of the regime as it moves towards increasing the use of coercive means against the Arab population. We must therefore give thought to finding a way to build the country so that the two national groups will be able to live alongside one another with a reasonable amount of mutual tolerance, sharing in the running of the country and in charting its course. The period preparatory for that must begin immediately.

This course of action has a positive and a negative aspect. The negative aspect is clear enough. The forms of discrimination still practiced in Israel against the Arab population must be abolished. Two forms of such discrimination deserve special note. Our citizenship law of 1952 lays down different naturalization procedures for Jews and non-Jews (by the latter, Arabs are mainly meant). The Jews are automatically citizens of Israel by force of "the Law of Return" while those Arabs who on census day in 1948 were for whatever reason not counted must undergo a naturalization process (or under some circumstances have it waived) subject to the discretion of the minister of the interior. That is why there are today several tens of thousands of Arabs who have been living in Israel legitimately and continuously since the very first days of the state, who nevertheless do not have Israeli citizenship.

Another form of discrimination is the matter of land expropriations. I will not enter here the tangle of legal arguments related to this matter, but I can call attention to the fact that the state's claim to ownership of lands held by Arab villagers is not always guileless. During the Mandate, when titles to real properties were being registered, the mandatory administration encountered the phenomenon of *mousha'a*, or collective ownership by the village of all or part of its lands (e.g., for grazing). In such instances it was not possible to register title to the land individually. The mandatory administration tried to solve this problem in various ways, ultimately by registering the village lands in the name of the high commissioner for the benefit of the village. Afterwards, on more than one occasion, the State of Israel claimed that that registration attested to state ownership of those lands. To do so is to mock the original intention of the registration and adds insult to the injury of the large-scale land seizures of the early fifties, which was accorded retroactive legal sanction by the Land Purchase (Approval of Actions and Compensations) Law — 1953.

In addition, there are other bothersome forms of discrimination unjustifiable on security grounds. The effort to keep Arabs from buying apartments in Upper Nazareth or in Carmiel does not stem from security needs but (and let us not mince words!) from racist narrow-mindedness. No less rankling is what has been done concerning customs benefits for returning Israelis. In December 1978 regulations were introduced stipulating that those entitled to such benefits have to meet a number of criteria, including: Israeli citizenship at the time of leaving and returning to Israel, and the second condition (which too has to be met!) — if the person did not have Israeli citizenship he has to have been entitled to it on the basis of the Law of Return.

That is a delicate way of saying that only Jews will be entitled to those benefits. Somebody apparently discovered several Arabs among the Israeli students returning to the country (not among the larger category of returnees, who until a short time ago also benefited from such customs concessions — namely, Israeli diplomats, and emissaries of the Jewish Agency and other institutions — for Arabs are not to be found among them). Disconcerted by the thought that the treasury was loosing a couple hundred thousand Israeli pounds each year because of those few Arab students, he prepared and issued these regulations, whose symbolic significance must arouse the ire of all those who hold democratic values dear.

All of these practices must be stopped immediately. An effort must be made in all realms of life and society to prevent all forms of discrimination against the Arabs of Israel that are not directly and clearly related to security needs (as long as the Arabs of Israel do not serve in the Israeli army, restrictions ensuing from security needs will be inevitable.) But beyond that, positive steps must also be taken. From its very inception Israel acknowledged that it is bicultural. Arabic is an official language and there is a state educational system that uses the Arabic language. This positive foundation must be developed and the potentialities it holds must in certain instances be unfolded. The Arab educational system must be accorded the same treatment, cultivation and resources as the Hebrew system. The Arabic language must become in fact the second official language. It is not enough that the name of the country appears in Arabic on our coins and bills. Every document, certificate, law, must be printed in both languages. The possibility of turning to the agencies of government and of law in Arabic and of receiving a reply in that language must be anchored in law and become an actual practice. It is an intolerable situation that road signs on most of Israel's highways are in Hebrew and English but not in Arabic. I know that most Israeli Arabs read Hebrew or English, and the absence of Arabic on road signs does not pose a real problem for them. Nevertheless, this matter has great symbolic importance. Whoever does not understand that should recall the struggle of the Yishuv during the Mandate period for the right to use Hebrew everywhere and for all purposes, even though it was clear that it was a matter of principle and not a practical matter. Symbols are very important. I have no doubt that when the Arabs of Israel become 30 percent of the population we will not be able to sustain the present symbols of the state, which stem only from Jewish tradition and culture — except if we are ready to accept full and total identification by the Arabs with national symbols that will come from the other side of the border.

In the field of education, ensuring the equality of Hebrew and Arabic education is not enough. An attempt should be made to achieve greater cooperation and even identity between the two systems, preserving only the language difference for those who want it. The program of instruction and textbooks must be based on a common humanistic and rationalistic foundation, with the common foundation expressed in each language in accord with the unique cultural tradition of each national group. In areas of mixed population, schools should be promoted in which Hebrew and Arab classes are housed together under one roof, in a joint educational-administrative framework.

Efforts should be made to eliminate frameworks that keep the members of the two national group apart. The Ottoman system of religious communities which requires every Israeli citizen to belong to a religious community in order to be able to marry, divorce and be buried must be abolished. The state must enact equal laws for all, enabling the establishment of a family without religious distinctions and eliminating the need for formal-legal distinctions between citizens on the basis of membership in a religious community.

The problem of the pressure on the land in the Galilee must be solved right away. A good deal of the frequent conflicts between Arab villagers and the state stem from the fact that the villages are growing and often there is not enough land for the young generation to earn a livelihood from agriculture or even on which to build living quarters. The solution of this problem requires rapid approval of master plans for the villages of the Galilee, the allotment of land for home construction and the acceleration of industrialization in order to lessen the pressure to obtain land for cultivation. One industrial undertaking can provide a livelihood for a population the size of an entire village, while requiring a tenth of the land necessary were those villagers to continue to earn their livelihood from agriculture. Industrialization may also ease the situation of thousands of workers who travel far from their villages daily, wasting much time and money on travels for which they get no return. If they decide to stay in the cities, close to their places of work, they generally have to sleep in rundown buildings not fit for human habitation, far from their family, estranged from their surroundings, often skidding towards violence and crime. This problem can also be solved by building housing near their places of employment for those workers who have established a permanent connection with places of employment in the cities. That would reduce the pressure on land in the Galilee and would solve the problem of tiring and expensive travel.

I believe that if we adopt this course we will lessen the tension between the two national groups in the country. If the peace process in the Middle East will advance at the same time, we will also be able to try to create a basis for real partnership in the state by the Arabs of Israel. To that end, we will all have to work, live, and educate so that the Israeli component in the collective identity of us all will be greater, while the ethnic-cultural component, that which links us to our past as Jews and Arabs, will become weaker. After we successfully get through this stage of psychological readiness, it will be necessary to bring the process to its culmination, namely, equality in bearing the burden of the country's defense. I have no doubt that without equality in this central realm of our life, we will not advance far; as long as there is still an important realm of life from which the Arabs of Israel are excluded, other limitations and restrictions will be derived from that, which it will be hard to confine within the bounds of security matters.

I do not agree with Rafi Israeli's proposal,* that the process of improving relations with the Arabs of Israel be begun by making them subject to compulsory military service. The obligation of military service and defense of the country against its enemies, who unfortunately happen to be members of the same people as the Israeli Arabs, can be demanded of the Israeli Arabs only on the basis of their full equality in a country where all doors are open to them. I have the distinct impression that those who demand that military service be immediately made obligatory for the Arabs of Israel, and who make Israeli citizenship conditional on the fulfilment of that obligation, are fully aware that the obligation will not be met and are actually looking for a way to deprive the Arabs of Israel of their Israeli citizenship. On the other hand, I say most frankly that it is necessary to arrive at that, but at the end of the process; if everything comes apart then, that will be proof that we have achieved nothing and had set out on the wrong course from the very beginning.

I suppose that it will be said against me that I have sketched an utopic vision that has no chance of being realized. That may be so. Nevertheless, it is best that we make an effort and try to take this course, for the alternative is an explosion and a conflagration that will engulf us all and mar beyond recognition the democratic and humanistic character of the State of Israel. Neither fate nor history has decreed that we must fail. Under circumstances not very different from those obtaining here, Finland successfully maintains harmonious relations with a national minority — the Swedes — who comprise 14 percent of its population, and who can look for inspiration, assistance

*   See p. 169.

and symbols of identification across the border to Sweden, which is immeasurably larger, stronger, and richer than Finland. But the full civil and cultural equality which the Swedish-speaking citizens genuinely enjoy has prevented the development of any incipient tendency of wanting to unite with fellow Swedes on the other side of the border, and prevented the formation of even the existence of a separate national-political identity (as distinct from an ethnic-cultural one). Everything I have proposed for Israel exists in Finland: separate educational systems for those who want them, joint educational institutions with separate classes, common education in Finnish for those who do not want separate education, full equality for the Swedish language at all levels of life (from restaurant menus to the most elaborate state documents) and full political freedom. There are Swedes who prefer to support parties on the basis of universal criteria and vote for conservatives, liberals, socialists, communists, etc., and there are those who prefer the Swedish party, which acts to protect Swedish particularist interests in Finland. Naturally, the obligations of citizenship, including defense of the country, are imposed equally on all. And as his name attests, the national hero of Finland and its leading defender in the winter war against the Russians in 1939–1940, General Mannerheim, was of Swedish origin.

ONE OUT OF EVERY SIX: A SUMMING UP

AVIGDOR LEVONTIN

In any discussion of the Arab minority in Israel, one must be careful to avoid smoothing down rough surfaces and embroidering matters in order to cloud reality. Loyalty to their country can, of course, be expected — even demanded — of the Arabs of Israel. Clearly, some of the Arab contributors to this book have offered even more than loyalty to Israel. In their remarks could be discerned a strain of identification with the state. This is eminently encouraging, but a certain qualification should be noted: the Arabs have always spoken — and that is only natural — of loyalty to, and identification with Israel, but not with its ends or with the vision for the sake of which it was established. They, of course, are not Zionists; nor should it be demanded of them that they become Zionists. We should bear in mind that a state is a means, an instrument, not an end. When the state is viewed as an end, fascism begins. By means of the state, however, it is possible to try to accomplish certain goals.

The Jewish people did not establish this state for the sake of having a state. It established Israel in order to achieve — through the agency of the state — certain things thought by many Jews to be desirable, such as the ingathering of the exiles. It is im-

possible to expect — indeed it is not expected, and would be in-
human and cruel to do so — that an Arab identify with the ends
or purpose of Israel, as distinct from identification with the state
itself. In other words, the optimal communion that can exist
between the Jewish majority and the Arab minority in Israel
would appear to be a partnership of body, not soul, nor a sharing
in the goal for which the state was established. The unalterable
truth must be faced that within our framework we do not have
the means to fulfill the Arab's national aspirations as distinct
from ensuring their civil rights and needs. It is within our power
to be fair towards the Arab citizens of our country. We can
acknowledge their full civil rights, but when it comes to national
rights —-that is a different matter. This state was not conceived
to answer Arab yearnings. It was designed to respond to a need
not theirs. The unadorned truth, in my view, is that not all of
the wishes of the Arabs, as individuals and as a group, can be
met within the framework of the State of Israel. We read here
of the dilemma faced by an Arab educator when an Arab
youngster tells him of his desire to become a pilot when he
grows up. The slogan is everywhere: "The best become flyers!"
The Arab educator, caught in a quandary, does not know what
to tell the boy. Should he say: "Yes, the best become flyers, but
that doesn't refer to you"? I think he should tell him the truth.
That is, for the foreseeable future it is very likely that an Arab
youngster who wants to be a pilot, especially an Air Force pilot,
will not be able to realize that dream in the State of Israel. As
already pointed out, not every Arab dream can be realized in
Israel. Perhaps the boy should also be told that the slogan is
used in recruitment propaganda for an army that in the past
fought against Arabs, and may be called upon to do so again in
the future.

And again, from time to time the thirst for agricultural land
intensifies. The question has been asked why Arab *moshavim*
have not been set up. I think — at least when used in reference
to land within the "Green Line" — expressions such as "national

domain" and "state land" and the like refer to land that, according to the Zionist conception and in accord with the ends for which this state was established, serves as a reserve for Jewish settlement; they do not imly that this land will be available in equal measure for setting up new Arab settlements; and so on.

Why do we not admit the truth to ourselves and say that between Jews and Arabs in Israel there is no dispute? The United Nations Charter is careful to distinguish between two concepts — "dispute" and "situation." Not all tension or rivalry between peoples is considered a "dispute." In the matter of a dispute, which is definable as such, you can also say: one side advances a certain argument and the other side raises a different argument, and someone must mediate between them. But not every situation can be clearly defined in terms of a dispute. Here we must be on our guard — our intellectual tools are honed mainly for dealing with disputes, not with situations. It is easy to deal with a dispute which is something clearly circumscribed. We are liable to be tempted to perceive situations as a dispute, which are not so at all. Israel's relationship to its Arab citizens is a situation, a state of affairs, and a difficult one, for which there in no pat soulution. It brings to mind the depth of insight of that wisest of men, the author of Ecclesiastes, in speaking of "that which is crooked" that "cannot be made straight." The assumption that there is no situation which men of "good will" cannot overcome is simply not true. There is also the crooked that cannot be made straight! There are situations that are not truly "soluble." We can be forthcoming towards our Arab citizens, who are our brothers in citizenship and in the state, we can meet them on the plane of civil rights, or participation in the state, but we cannot, within our national framework, satisfy their national aspirations. This is a hard truth to face, but an essential one.

This situation forces me to question the rosy future envisaged by Yehoshua Porath with regard to the possibility of a melting pot in this region. The archetype of the melting pot is the United

States as it was perceived until not long ago, before the melting pot stopped melting, or slowed down. What characterizes the American melting pot is that even the majority, the Protestants of Anglo-Saxon origin, were ready to take part in, or be exposed to, the melting process. They came to the United States with a readiness — however qualified and however tentative — to turn their backs on their past and to begin a new adventure, to become "American." The majority after, say, two generations were ready to stop being Britons and Scotsmen and to begin to be Americans. The Jews, however, did not come to Israel in order to stop being Jews. They came to Israel largely to revive their Jewishness. This was the Jewish renaissance. A renaissance suggests facing a future, true, but also drawing on a past. You don't try to shape an unknown, adventurous future, by groping your way towards it. Here, we are speaking of the revival of a particular historical heritage. Not all the Jews came here for that, but many did. For those Jews the metaphor of the melting pot is not applicable. I would go one step further and say that it is not applicable in the case of our Arab citizens either. Such a vision does not do them justice or pay them due honor. I don't think they will agree, nor is it even proper to propose that they renounce their Arabness so that together we can create some new "Israeli" entity. That, it seems to me, is simply not possible. Through a process of elimination we find ourselves perhaps not in a hopeless state but at any rate without a single, sweeping, saving formula. For there is no such formula.

However, and especially in light of the radicalization in both camps, other motifs are appearing, some of which came to the fore here. I think that at least at the centers of the two camps, though not at their fringes, among sober people, the recognition has grown that we have no choice but to get along together — not because we are enamored of the idea, or enamored of each other, but because there is no alternative. The price that will have to be paid — by both sides — in order to persist in not getting along, is utterly unacceptable. Actually, there is no price. It is possible not to get along, but given the circumstances of time and place, "to persist in not getting along" is a contradiction in terms. Incidentally, I do not think that to "get along" has derogatory implications as someone suggested. To get along or get by is at times the art most necessary for survival. Our separate histories mean that each of us has arrived in the State of Israel heavily burdened with his distinct historic load. Arabness, Islam, are great, deep-rooted and powerful cultural forces. They are one of the great components of universal history. A Jew may be allowed to say that he views Judaism in the same way. That being the case, each of us enters this state carrying his own cultural baggage, with a tendency to stress his group's particularity, irreversibly separating him from his partner in this state. All of these forces push us towards confrontation and polarization. But here a countervailing force seems to appear on the horizon, one that may yet save the situation. Along with the deep atavistic urges and the particularistic cultural heritage, comes the elemental need to survive. Without life there is no particularist cultural heritage or zeal or even hatred.

This need to survive impels us towards accommodations and relaxation of tension, towards détente and the understanding that we must get along together. In plain terms, in the situation existing today in the world and around us the Jews and the Arabs are in a certain sense each other's hostage. Furthermore, it seems that in this nuclear age mankind as a whole is the hostage of both these groups.

A large question that still remains unanswered, which has not been dealth with explicitly in this collection, is how to achieve a relaxation of the tension between Jews and Arabs in Israel. Is integration better, or will crowding together, working together, coming to "know" one another, increase tension? Perhaps it is better for reducing tension that we be cooler and more restrained, maintaining some distance from one another. We may recall the cautionary slogan we used to see along Israel's highways about keeping a distance in order to prevent accidents. Consideration should also be given to the virtues of distance. And that brings me to my final comment.

If the Arab minority is truly able to attain civil and human fulfillment but not full national satisfaction in Israel, it may be that in the future we will have to give serious thought to devising special frameworks not necessarily confined within Israel's borders but which may also be, perhaps partially, trans-national, federative, confederative, and within which the Arabs in Israel may be able to find some relief on the national as distinct from the civil plane. Here I have allowed myself to speculate about things to come.

LIST OF CONTRIBUTORS

Hana Abu-Hana	The Arab Orthodox College, Haifa
Jalal Abu-Ta'ama	Member of the local council of Baqa Al-Gharbiya
Zeidan Atashi	'Isfiya; former member of the Knesset
Avraham Burg	Student, Jerusalem
David Glass	Lawyer; former member of the Knesset
Alouph Hareven	The Van Leer Jerusalem Foundation
Elias Houri	Lawyer, Jerusalem
Rafi Israeli	The Truman Institute, The Hebrew University of Jerusalem
George Kanazi	Department of Arab Language and Literature, Haifa University
Avigdor Levontin	School of Law, The Hebrew University of Jerusalem
Atallah Mansour	Writer and journalist, Nazareth
Mahmoud Miari	Bir-Zeit University
Yehoshua Porath	The Institute of Asian and African Studies, The Hebrew University of Jerusalem
Eli Rekhess	The Shiloah Center for Middle Eastern Studies, Tel-Aviv University
Saad Sarsour	Youth Department, Ministry of Education and Culture, Nazareth
Anton Shammas	Writer and poet, Jerusalem
Sammy Smooha	Department of Sociology, Haifa University
Muhammad Wattad	Member of the Knesset; educator and journalist

THE VAN LEER JERUSALEM FOUNDATION SERIES